A

MARTYR

SOUL

REMEMBERED

Detail from the Monument de la Réformation in the
Promenade des Bastions, showing (left to right)
Guillaume Farel, John Calvin, Theodore Beza, and
John Knox

A MARTYR SOUL REMEMBERED:

COMMEMORATING
THE 450TH ANNIVERSARY OF

THE DEATH OF MICHAEL SERVETUS

**GENEVA
24TH–27TH OCTOBER 2003**

EDITED BY Clifford M. Reed

Prague, Czech Republic
International Council of Unitarians and Universalists
2004

ISBN (paperback): 0-9723134-1-9

Reed, Clifford M., 1947–
   A martyr soul remembered : commemorating the
450th anniversary of the death of Michael Servetus / [an
ICUU conference held in] Geneva 24th–27th October
2003 / edited by Clifford M. Reed. / Foreword by Jill K.
McAllister. [Kalamazoo, Michigan] : ICUU, 2004.
   xxii, 240 p.
   Includes references and index.
   1. Servetus, Michael (1511–1553)—Memorials   I.
Title II. Hawkes, Henry Warburton, 1843–1917 III.
Rzepka, Jane R., 1950 – IV. Sütő, Andras, 1927– V.
International Council of Unitarians and Universalists
BX9869 .S4 R44 2003   921 .S489 R44

Printed by Fidlar Doubleday, Inc.
Kalamazoo, Michigan

CONTENTS

FOREWORD – Jill McAllister   xi

PREFACE – Clifford M. Reed   xv

THE CONTRIBUTORS   xx

THE PROGRAMME

Friday, 24th October—The keynote address   1
   Michael Servetus: one of us –
     Clifford M. Reed   3

Saturday, 25th October   21
   The influence of Michael Servetus on
   Francis Dávid and the beginnings of
   Transylvanian Unitarianism –
     Elek Rezi   23

   Why Unitarians and Universalists owe
   more to John Calvin than they do to
   Michael Servetus –
     Andrew M. Hill   41

   Servetus as sacrifice –
     Peter Hughes   69

Sunday, 26th October   101
   Servetus, science, and the Breath of God:
   honouring Servetus in 2003, a sermon –
     Richard Boeke   103

Sunday, 26th October, continued
Servetus in Geneva: places to visit –
    Clifford M. Reed   115

The Servetus monument, Geneva –
    Andrew M. Hill   121

The drama of Servetus –
    Clifford M. Reed   127

Appendix 1. *Servetus: a drama* –
    Henry Warburton Hawkes   136

Appendix 2. *The diary of Catalina
Conesa* –
    Jane Rzepka   145

Appendix 3. *Csillag a maglyan [Flames
at the stake]* –
    Andras Sütõ, transl. Alan Williams   157

Monday 27th October   177
A service to commemorate the 450th
anniversary of the martyrdom of Michael
Servetus (1511–1553), theologian and
physician, held at Champel, Geneva   179

ADDITIONAL MATERIALS   189
    Appendix 4. Michael's meditations:
    prayers and meditations based on,

ADDITIONAL MATERIALS, *continued*
    inspired by or drawn from the writings
    of Michael Servetus –
        Clifford M. Reed   191

Appendix 5. A hymn for Michael
    Servetus –
        Andrew M. Hill   207

Appendix 6. Conference attendees   209

Appendix 7. International Council
    of Unitarians and Universalists   211

SOURCE INDEX   213

SUBJECT INDEX   218

A Martyr Soul Remembered

FOREWORD

— ~ —

Some years ago, my colleague Mark Morrison Reed, a Unitarian Universalist minister and recent past president of the Canadian Unitarian Council, wrote these words:

> The religious community is essential,
> for alone our vision is too narrow to
> see all that must be seen, and our strength
> too limited to do all that must be done.
> Together, our vision widens and our
> strength is renewed.*

They express for me both the essence and the promise of the International Council of Unitarians and Universalists (ICUU). In fact, they express my deepest convictions about the ongoing search for truth and wisdom. No matter how much one has learned, no matter how wide one's own experience and insight, it is simply not possible for one individual to

* **"The Task of the Religious Community," no. 580 in** *Singing the Living Tradition*, **Beacon Press and The Unitarian Universalist Association, 1993.**

hold all that can be considered truth. No matter how powerful, no matter how sure of its own perspective and priorities, it is simply not possible for one country or group or organization to hold all that can be considered true and right and good.

This is true for all Unitarian Universalists (U / U's) in our various organizations and institutions around the world. We each have our own perspectives—our own particular history and traditions, our own practices and preferences, our own dreams and dilemmas, our own social, political and economic context—which make the truths we hold for ourselves unique in some ways. Yet, like the blind men in the ancient Hindu story, who can describe only the parts of an elephant that they individually experience, the unique perspectives, experiences, and insights of any one group do not, and cannot, encompass the whole of who we are.

When U / U's from around the world meet together to explore and study and uphold our common religious heritage and values, what always seems to happen is that, "our vision widens and our strength is renewed." This happens at ICUU Council meetings when we decide on projects and policies for mutual aid and support. It happens in leadership training conferences where we share organizational experience and expertise. It happens in study tours where we learn about the daily life and religious practices of other member groups. It happens whenever we worship together, and it happens in programs and symposia like the event that honored the 450th anniversary of the death of Michael Servetus, held in Geneva in October 2003.

At these times, our pluralism is the vehicle for our growth and learning: a source of new understanding and new vision, a source of challenge and strength for each of us. When we study and work together, we create opportunities to see and respect our differences. Our understanding of what we have in common increases, and our appreciation for the broader scope of who we are as U / U's grows. This is pluralism in action. This is a model for a world of diverse individuals and groups who still must find ways to live peacefully and sustainably together, helping one another.

These papers and proceedings from the 2003 ICUU conference commemorating the death of Michael Servetus are inspirational. They draw us to revisit a common point in our histories, and they lead us to re-examine a story that, like all mythology, can easily be oversimplified and underappreciated. They open new windows of perspective on our understanding of our religious history, inviting us to see new sides of the story, to acknowledge different interpretations. They compel us to remember the sacrifice of a human being, in the most excruciating way, and to acknowledge how that very real sacrifice affects our lives today.

The success of the conference, and the quality of these proceedings, points the way for our continued work and study together in the future. There is so much for us to explore and to share as we tell the stories of who we are, and as we dream the dreams of who we want to be. Wherever we live, we all face the questions of how to best live our religious lives, and how to make our liberal religious communities places of vital engagement with the world to help bring about the unity, and peace, and justice that we dream of. "...[A]lone our vision is too narrow to see all that must be seen, and our strength too limited to do all that must be done. Together, our vision widens and our strength is renewed."

Thanks to all who participated, who studied and presented, and who took these questions to heart for U / U's in many countries. I look forward to all of the work we have yet to share.

Jill McAllister
Past President
International Council of Unitarians and Universalists

PREFACE

— ~ —

In October 2003, Unitarians and Unitarian Universalists from Europe and America gathered in Geneva to commemorate the martyrdom of Michael Servetus. Over the course of four days—from the 24th to the 27th—we listened to academic papers, we visited the 'Servetus sites' in the old city, we heard dramatic readings about Servetus, and we held services of worship. Our purpose was to learn more about this remarkable and still controversial Spanish 'heretic,' and to consider his theological, spiritual and historical significance for today's Unitarian and Unitarian Universalist faith-community. We wanted to pay tribute to his part in the origins of our tradition and to remember his courage and his suffering, but not in terms of a simplistic hero worship.

Our company comprised a wide range, from scholars with a deep knowledge of Servetus to those who came with a more limited acquaintance. This made for a fascinating mix, all the more so for being drawn from several different nationalities. The commemoration was organised by the International Council of Unitarians and Universalists, which felt that the 450th anniversary of Servetus's death by burning should not pass unmarked by the religious community that owes him most.

Although the event was primarily a Unitarian and Unitarian Universalist gathering, it also had an important ecumenical component. The conference centre where we were so handsomely accommodated belongs to the Reformed Protestant Church and is named after John Knox. Our main Sunday worship was held in a nearby Protestant Church, the Chapelle des Crêts, where we were welcomed warmly by pastor and congregation. And at our commemorative worship in Champel on 27th October we were joined by the local pastor and two senior officials of the Protestant Church of Geneva. It was good to recall together the tragic event that had taken place there exactly four and a half centuries previously.

This book brings you the record of that weekend in Geneva. It is the hope of the ICUU that it will not only make more permanent our commemoration of this 'martyr soul,' but that it will be a resource for your own study, reflection and worship on the theme of Michael Servetus.

Acknowledgements
Although extending thanks to people always runs the risk of leaving somebody out, I would, nevertheless, like to express my gratitude to the following:

— Christine Hayhurst, my conference co-organiser without whose sterling work and unfailing support the event in Geneva would never have happened. Christine has served the Unitarian cause in a great many capacities over the years and replaced me on the ICUU Executive Committee in May 2003. She is a member of the Unitarian congregation in Godalming, Surrey, England.

— Diane Worden of WordenDex Plus in Kalamazoo, Michigan, without whose expertise, enthusiasm and hard work this book would never have happened, and Holley Lantz for her professional input. Special mention should also be made of their work on composite photographs and graphics creation. Holley and Diane are members of People's Church in Kalamazoo. Also, those whose support have made publication possible.

— Cornelia Pomiersky and Marc Appel of the Centre International Reformé John Knox, for all that they did before and during the event to ensure its success and our comfort.

— Pasteur Daniel Neeser and the congregation at Chapelle des Crêts, for their hospitality and their welcome at our Sunday morning service in Geneva. The Rt. Rev. Joel Stroudinsky, president of the Protestant Church of Geneva, for his words at the Servetus Memorial. Mme. Marianne

Wanstall, the Protestant Church's regional president, and Pasteur Marie-Laure Jakubec of the Champel-Malagnou parish for being there too.

— Elaine Carlson and Thomas Murray of the Unitarian Universalist fellowship in Geneva for their support and assistance during the planning stages—especially on one formidably hot August day when no one in their right mind should have been wandering around the city! Dorothée Reumann of Geneva Tourism for her invaluable guidance.

— Beryl Beech of the Ipswich Unitarian Meeting for finding the Old Town map and the prints of 16th century Geneva. These appeared in *The Little Book of Geneva,* by B. Bradfield, published by the Librairie Kundig, Geneva, in 1926. I have been unable to trace either the publisher or further details of the author.

— Our speakers, the Rev. Dr. Elek Rezi, the Rev. Andrew Hill and the Rev. Dr. Peter Hughes, for their erudition and their words. The Rev. Dr. Richard Boeke for his Sunday morning service and for his unfailing advice, support and dedication. Those who led our morning and evening devotions: the Rev. Austin Fitzpatrick (2003–04 president of the General Assembly of Unitarian and Free Christian Churches), the Revs.

Celia and John Midgley, Esther Hurlburt and the Rev. Cynthia Cain, and Eloise Mayo.

— Alan Williams, not only for his translation of Andras Sütõ's play and permission to reproduce excerpts from it, but also for his efforts to get the permission of Mr. Sütõ and his publishers, to whom I am also very grateful. The Rev. Dr. Jane Rzepka, minister of the UUA's Church of the Larger Fellowship, for permission to use her *Diary of Catalina Conesa* and to include it in this book.

— Esther Hurlburt, Richard Boeke and Paulette Reed for allowing us to use their photographs. The Michael Servetus Institute and the Servetus International Society for their help in locating artworks, and their granting permission for us to include them or helping us to get it. The drawing of Servetus by Pablo Picasso is reproduced by permission of the Artists Rights Society, New York, with special thanks to Maria Fernanda Meza for her help.

— All those who contributed to the worship, the dramatic readings and the interchange of ideas that made the event a fitting commemoration of Michael Servetus and his legacy.

Clifford M. Reed
Editor and Conference Co-organiser

THE CONTRIBUTORS
— ~ —

Richard Boeke is a Unitarian Universalist minister living in southern England. He has served churches in both the USA and the UK and is currently minister at Horsham, West Sussex. He was secretary of ICUU from 1997 to 2001 and is currently president of the World Congress of Faiths.

Andrew M. Hill is minister of St. Mark's Unitarian Church in Edinburgh, Scotland. A leading historian of British Unitarianism, he is a former secretary of the Unitarian Historical Society and author of *A Liberal Religious Heritage: Unitarian & Universalist foundations in Europe, America & elsewhere.* At ICUU's Symposium 2001, he gave a paper on, "The Unitarian and Universalist World 1901 to 2001: Seven Strands," and was principal editor of the proceedings.

Peter Hughes is a Unitarian Universalist minister and vice president of the Unitarian Universalist Historical Society. He is chief editor of the on-line Dictionary of

Unitarian and Universalist Biography. Although mainly concerned with Universalist history, he has a particular interest in Servetus. With Lynn Hughes, he has been working on a reprint of Roland H. Bainton's definitive 1953 biography, *Hunted Heretic: the life and death of Michael Servetus, 1511–1553.*

Jill K. McAllister is minister of People's Church, Kalamazoo, Michigan. She was ICUU's president from 1999 to 2003 and its treasurer from 1995 to 1999. Jill is also a former first vice moderator of the Unitarian Universalist Association, and she co-edited *A Global Conversation* (ICUU, 2002).

Clifford M. Reed is a Unitarian minister in Ipswich, Suffolk, England. He was the first secretary of ICUU (1995–97) and continued to serve on the Executive Committee until May 2003. He was the 1997–98 president of the General Assembly of Unitarian and Free Christian Churches. He chaired the organising committee of the ICUU's "Symposium 2001: Unitarian / Universalism at the Dawn of the 21st Century," held at Harris Manchester College, Oxford. With Andrew Hill and Jill McAllister, he co-edited the proceedings, published by ICUU as *A Global Conversation.*

Elek Rezi is deputy bishop of the Unitarian Church of Transylvania and dean of the Unitarian theological faculty at the Protestant Seminary in Cluj (Koloszvar), Romania. He has served on the ICUU

Executive Committee (1997–99) and he spoke on, "Transylvanian Unitarian Theology at the Dawn of the New Century," at the ICUU's Symposium 2001.

~

A Martyr Soul Remembered:
Commemorating the 450th Anniversary of the
Death of Michael Servetus

DAY I

Friday, 24th October 2003

— ~ —

EVENING: Centre International Reformé
John Knox

A Martyr Soul Remembered

MICHAEL SERVETUS: ONE OF US

Clifford M. Reed
Minister, Ipswich Unitarian Meeting, Suffolk

— ~ —

On behalf of the International Council of
Unitarians and Universalists, I welcome you the John
Knox International Reformed Centre and to this
weekend of commemoration for Michael Servetus.

There is, of course, no little irony in our meeting
in a place dedicated to one of John Calvin's most
faithful lieutenants! John Knox preached the Calvinist
Reformation in Scotland and had a profound
influence on that nation's history and character.

But we are not here* to remember Knox, but
rather someone of whom he most thoroughly
disapproved, namely Michael Servetus, Michel
Servet, Miguel Serveto. Did their paths cross? Not

** Geneva was once a city of refuge for persecuted Protestants.
It was home to Voltaire and the League of Nations, and it still
houses offices of many international organisations. But for
Unitarian / Universalists, Geneva is inextricably linked with
the cruel death of a forerunner of our faith tradition.*

that I've ever heard or read, though others here may know more of this than I do. It is interesting, though, that at the time when Michael Servetus was in flight from the French Inquisition in the summer of 1553, John Knox was in flight from England. There, on 6th July, Mary Tudor—'bloody' Mary as she was to become known—had succeeded to the English throne. And she had a personal mission! It was to undo the Protestant Reformation of her father, Henry VIII, and more especially of her brother, Edward VI. She was to undo it with blood and fire.

Knox had found asylum in Edward's England, but this was now at an end. As a refugee he set out for Calvin's Geneva, where his reception must have been very different to that of Servetus! As to whether their time here overlapped, I don't know. Knox lived to return in triumph to his native land, but Servetus was not to be so fortunate. Such a notorious heretic struck fear, horror and even hatred into the hearts of the so-called 'orthodox'. Two hundred thirty-six years later, a Scottish poet with strong Unitarian sympathies wrote words that seem appropriate to Servetus, although written in defence of later religious liberals:

> Orthodox, orthodox,
> Wha believe in John Knox,
> Let me sound an alarm to your conscience,
> There's a heretic blast
> Has been blawn i' the wast,
> That what is not sense must be nonsense.

The poet was, of course, Robert Burns, and the poem, "The Kirk's Alarm".

Michael Servetus had concluded that the doctrine of the Trinity as taught by the Roman Catholic Church, and as retained by the major Protestant Reformers of the 16th century, was, in Burns' words, "not sense" and therefore "must be nonsense".

It was his challenge to the idea of a Trinity of Persons, distinct yet of 'one substance', that first brought the precocious and contentious Spanish youth, Miguel Serveto, to the disapproving attention of Catholic and Protestant alike. His first book, *De Trinitatis Erroribus—On the Errors of the Trinity* published in 1531, and his second, *Dialogorum de Trinitate Libri Duo—Two Dialogues on the Trinity* published the following year, were soon to make him a marked man, Bainton's *Hunted Heretic.*

Servetus had made a frontal assault on the Catholic and creedal doctrine of God. He had forced into the open an issue that the Reformation's leaders preferred to keep quiet. Many of them knew perfectly well that Servetus's arguments from Scripture were cogent ones, especially after Erasmus had discredited the one 'proof' text of the Trinity, I John 5:7, in his Greek New Testament of 1516.

At one point Calvin himself was to be accused— by one Petrus Caroli—of "complicity with

Arianism"! And maybe this is why Protestants were at least as hostile to Servetus as Catholics. As François Wendel wrote in his study of Calvin, "…it was the memory of Caroli's insinuations that led [Calvin] afterwards to insist so strongly upon the trinitarian dogma." Wendel adds, "…perhaps it also played a part in his attitude towards Servetus." Protestant leaders, and a Catholic reformer such as Erasmus, preferred to leave the Trinity alone, lest they be accused of departing from the historic creeds of Christianity. Servetus was rocking the boat, a boat in which they did not feel very secure.

Should Servetus have just shut up about it, as he was so firmly advised to do? Well, no, he shouldn't. It was a matter of intellectual and religious honesty. How could a Church, supposedly founded on Scripture, retain and enshrine as 'divine truth' a doctrine of God that was alien to Scripture; and which contradicted the witness of Scripture with regard both to God and to Jesus Christ? Whatever our view today of the nature and status of the Bible, in the context of 16th-century Europe, Servetus was making a stand for honesty and for scholarship, over against dishonesty and wilful ignorance. This was not appreciated by those whose consciences were troubled by what he wrote.

And so began the saga of Michael Servetus as a theologian of the Radical Reformation. Reaction to his early works was so hostile that, before long, he wore out his welcome with even those more tolerant Reformers with whom he sought refuge and debate, such as Johannes Oecolompadius in Basel. And it should be said that he was not one to mince his words in the fiery and abusive exchanges of 16th-century disputation! But in the end things were getting just too hot, and Servetus disappeared. He just dropped out of sight for 20 years.

At the same time as Michael Servetus vanished from the scene, a young man named Michel de Villeneuve appeared in France. During the next two decades he worked with distinction as an editor. He studied mathematics and medicine in Paris, although he had to leave the city for a time because of religious and political tensions—as did another young scholar named Jean Cauvin (John Calvin) with whom he nearly met to discuss theology.

Back in Paris, de Villeneuve studied anatomy and it may well have been at this point that he discovered some previously unknown and revolutionary facts about the pulmonary circulation of the blood. He also wrote a highly successful book on the medical use of syrups (*Syruporum Universa Ratio,* 1537), and clashed with the University authorities over his apparent support for 'judicial' astrology—the use of astrology to predict the future. This interest may seem strange to us, but at the time astrology and astronomy were more or less inextricable, and few doubted the link between earthly and heavenly events. Servetus moved between Paris, Charlieu and Lyons, to work, and finally he settled in Vienne, a town on the Rhone. Here he became a respected and respectable medical practitioner. And besides his work as a doctor, he continued as an editor, notably of Ptolemy's *Geography* (1535, 1541) and of the so-called 'Pagnini Bible' (1542–45).

To the astute observer, de Villeneuve's work as an editor revealed more about him than met the eye. And de Villeneuve himself, spurred on by this work and by the driving honesty that had filled the young Servetus—for, of course, it was he—returned to his first love, theology. He wrote a new book. This great and definitive work, *Christianismi Restitutio (The Restoration of Christianity),* was finally printed, in cloak-and-dagger circumstances in September 1552. But suspicions had already been aroused—notably in Calvin's Geneva—that Michel de Villeneuve was none other than the notorious heretic, Michael Servetus. An ecumenical conspiracy was born with the sole purpose of exposing, entrapping and destroying him. It brought together in unlikely alliance, the Roman Catholic Inquisition in France and John Calvin in Protestant Geneva.

The contents of the *Christianismi Restitutio* were hardly likely to improve the situation. All the old Servetian 'heresies' were there with plenty more besides! To the brash passion of youth were added the fruits of 20 years of further wide-ranging scholarship.

He had produced a powerful challenge to 'orthodoxy' that neither Catholic nor Protestant could ignore.

The book barely survived the concerted effort to extirpate it from the face of the Earth. Ironically, it seems to be the case that the only three copies to have survived were those owned personally by Servetus's bitterest enemies for the purposes of convicting him. One of these was Calvin's. It is believed to be the one that now resides in Edinburgh, where John Knox held sway in St. Giles' Cathedral in the years following Servetus's death.

And so the tragedy unfolds: arrest in France, escape, flight and finally an ill-starred arrival in Geneva in August 1553. He lodged at the Rose d'Or inn on the corner of rue du Rhône and the Place du Molard. Then arrest in the Temple de la Madeleine, followed by imprisonment and a show trial in the old Bishop's Palace, L'Évêché, which served as a courthouse and none-too-salubrious jail. Condemnation as a heretic came on 26th October. Death, by burning at the stake at Champel, came the following day at noon. It is this martyrdom that we are here to commemorate this weekend, 450 years on.

But why should we, as Unitarians and Universalists, claim Servetus as a martyr for our faith and our tradition? It has been said that, really, he had little to do with our faith; that he was not really a

Unitarian—let alone a Universalist—and that our interest in him is limited to the issues of religious freedom and tolerance that his case raised.

Now, of course, these are very important issues. The case of Servetus brought them to prominence, notably through Sebastian Castellio's seminal work, *De Haereticis (Concerning Heretics)*, of 1554. Castellio (or Castellion) too had felt the wrath of Calvin and been forced to flee Geneva as a result. But I think we do Servetus an injustice if we restrict his relevance to his 'case' rather than include his ideas and beliefs as well. Within the teachings of this remarkable and courageous Spaniard is much that speaks to us today, and which may have been more influential that it is sometimes given credit for.

In him, I think, we really do see a pioneer of our Unitarian and Universalist tradition, someone on whose shoulders we stand, someone who—in the community of time—is 'one of us'. Very briefly, let me touch on at least ten reasons why I think so:

1. Oneness of God

His prime theological concern was to maintain the true Oneness of God, the same monotheism to which the Bible witnesses. In opposition to 'orthodox' theology, with its Trinity of semi-independent and co-equal 'persons,' Servetus affirmed the strict Unity of God. He said that the terms "Father, Son and Holy Spirit" refer simply to 'dispositions' of God, that is, ways in which God operates or in which God is apprehended and perceived. Rather than there being three divine 'persons' sharing one 'substance', there is but one divine reality—one divine substance—known conventionally as the 'Father,' from whom all else proceeds or emanates.

To the modern mind these subtleties are hard to comprehend. What Servetus was doing, however, was to replace a doctrine that, whatever the caveats, divided God into three and so effectively made three gods. In its place he proposed an uncompromising monotheism, but one which still recognised that God comes to us in various ways at various times, works in various ways and is approached by various means.

2. Humanity of Jesus

Although Servetus accepted the 'miraculous' birth of Christ, it being a scriptural doctrine, he was at pains to stress that Jesus was a man, and as such should not be swallowed up by the theology that had arisen around him.

Rather than Jesus being a pre-existent divine being in human form, he was a true man—albeit fathered by God—who received an 'inward anointing' which conferred divinity upon his spirit. Thus he was the Christ, the Anointed One. God effected this through the agency of the Holy Spirit, which refers simply to the means by which God worked and not to a distinct divine being or 'person.'

The Holy Spirit was thus the activity of God in the anointing or divinisation of the spirit of Jesus the human being. And although this may seem to separate Jesus from the rest of humanity, Servetus went on to say that, "the Holy Spirit is the activity of God in the spirit of man" *(cf., On the Errors of the Trinity),* and, indeed, it is only in the human spirit that the Holy Spirit can be said to be active at all.

Thus the same Holy Spirit with which God anointed Jesus and made him the Christ, is also God's active presence in ourselves. Jesus Christ may be the inwardly anointed "Son of the Eternal God," as Servetus called him at Champel, but it is an anointing in which, to a degree, we all share. Thus the divine and the human mingle in all of us, as they did supremely in Jesus the Anointed.

3. All in God, God in all

Following on from Servetus's view of Jesus Christ is what has been called his 'pantheism'. Personally, I think 'panentheism' might be a better term. Pantheism identifies all reality with God, whereas panentheism means that all things are in God and God is in all things.

Servetus argued that there is one undivided God, but not that God is locked into the fabric of the universe as if set in concrete! God remains subtle and active and greater than the created universe. God contains and enfolds the universe, while also pervading it—present and active in all things. Divine essence and activity are neither confined to Jesus nor even to the rest of humankind, but are poured out to be present in every animal and plant, every river and every rock. God's Unity can be discerned in the oneness, interconnectedness and interrelatedness of the Creation.

4. Universal salvation

Servetus advanced the radical idea that there is salvation outside Christianity. He argued, at least with respect to people who live beyond the range of Christendom, that their good deeds, done in response to the natural promptings of conscience, will be acceptable on the Day of Judgment. Conscience is a divinely implanted and universal human characteristic. Thus the possibility of salvation is open to all human beings, whether Christian or not. Servetus can thus be seen as a pioneer of Universalism as well as of Unitarianism!

5. Inherent innocence

Servetus had an elevated view of human nature very much in contrast with that of his theological opponents, especially Calvin. Not only did he see the human spirit as being indwelt by the Divine Spirit, he also said that our sins are only—and can only be— acquired after the innocence of childhood and even youth. Sin and sinfulness are not innate or predetermined.

We are not tainted by inherited guilt on account of 'original sin'. Our sins—though real enough!—are our own business and responsibility, to be dealt with by personal repentance and the forgiveness that God holds out in Christ. The Divine Word speaks in him to draw us closer to God, to the divine within ourselves.

Thus we may die to our sinful self and rise with Christ to a new kind of life that is not conditioned by death. Servetus still saw Christ and his sacrifice as crucial to salvation for those who know about him, but the means of gaining it are available to all. Indeed, those means are closer than we can possibly imagine, for our own inward selves are divine. We are as Christ was, if only we will allow ourselves to be freed from the numbing of the heart, the defrauding of the brain and the inebriating of the senses, that Servetus ascribed to the machinations of the Devil!

6. Monotheistic sympathies

Servetus had a radical attitude to other faiths, with a particular sympathy for the other great monotheistic faiths, Judaism and Islam. As a Spaniard, he was familiar with both of these, and with the appalling persecutions to which Jews and Muslims had been subjected in Catholic Spain. As himself a persecuted upholder of monotheism, in the face of what he saw as its denial by the Church, he could not help but have

14

sympathy for the Inquisition's Jewish and Muslim victims.

Servetus was, of course, fully conversant with the Jewish Bible, known to Christians as the Old Testament. He had also read the Qur'an. Although not published in Latin until 1543, translations in manuscript form must have been available before this, especially in Spain. It may well be that Servetus knew Arabic. There was an old tradition—not given much credence these days—that Servetus had even travelled to North Africa, whence the Moors had retreated from Spain, to study Islam at first hand.

Servetus saw the 'orthodox' doctrine of the Trinity as an insuperable barrier between Christianity and its sister-faiths. As a Christian, he had criticisms of both Judaism and Islam, but at least he recognised that all three faiths worshipped the same One God. He accorded a degree of validity to Islam and Judaism that 'orthodox' Christianity did not, and he shared their criticism and rejection of the doctrine of the Trinity. To remove the Trinity from the equation, to restore a truly monotheistic theology, might enable the old barriers to come down and—in Servetus's vision—allow Jew and Muslim to accept a restored and reformed Christianity. It wasn't, of course, interfaith relationships as we might envisage them today, but it was a very significant advance on the violent bigotry that institutional Christianity had displayed until then! And for a long time afterwards, it must be said.

Appropriately, a modern Muslim view of Servetus (in *Jesus: A Prophet of Islam,* by Muhammad 'Ata-ur-Rahmin) sees him as one of those Christians who came closest to the Islamic view of God and of Jesus, focusing on his reference to Jesus as 'the prophet' in *On the Errors of the Trinity.*

7. Disagreement without violence

Servetus, although a robust and contentious advocate of his beliefs, did not display a desire to treat his theological opponents as they wanted to treat him—and did once they got the chance. Eirenic exchanges of views were not the norm in 16th-century theological debate, and Servetus gave as good as he got in this regard. But when it came to the question of how to deal with those with whom one disagreed, Servetus clearly and specifically rejected violence and death.

To kill others because of their beliefs, their interpretation of Scripture or their mistakes was unacceptable. Servetus wrote in a letter,

> I consider it a very serious matter to kill a
> man simply because he may be mistaken
> in some question of interpretation of the
> scripture, knowing that even the most

knowledgeable ones may also fall into error.

Servetus, hunted and condemned to death by Catholic and Protestant alike, showed himself to be on the road to that advocacy of the rights of conscience which were to become a central affirmation of the later Unitarian and Universalist movements.

8. Scientific search for truth and meaning

Servetus was a pioneer of that reconciliation of science and religion, that use of the scientific method in the search for truth and meaning, which became characteristic of the Unitarian and Universalist traditions.

In medicine he made significant contributions, the greatest of which was his discovery and description of the pulmonary circulation of the blood. If *Christianismi Restitutio*—in which the description appeared—had not been so thoroughly suppressed, one wonders how much human suffering might have been prevented. European medicine would have been nearly a century further on in this area by the time William Harvey came on the scene. Servetus also made contributions in geography (the two editions of Ptolemy) and astronomy, his dabblings in astrology notwithstanding!

9. Rational scholarship and inquiry

Servetus's determination to restore Christianity to its original monotheistic purity went hand in hand with a deep and uncompromising commitment to sound scholarship.

Whether in Biblical studies, theology or medicine—all interrelated in his panentheistic understanding—his object was to uncover the truth, even though this meant confronting established 'orthodoxies'. He thus helped to stimulate that tradition of radical questioning and rational inquiry in all areas of knowledge which was to become a major aspect of our movement. Servetus always saw this in terms of his faith, the rational going hand in hand with the spiritual, as do we.

10. Rights of conscience

And finally there is the matter of his 'case'. As a prisoner of conscience and a martyr for his—and our—faith, Servetus became a cogent symbol in the long struggle for religious liberty, tolerance and the rights of conscience. He was, indeed, 'one of us,' and we have many reasons to commemorate him.

~

SOURCES

'ATA-UR-RAHMIN, Muhammad. *Jesus: A Prophet of Islam.* 3rd edition. London: MWH London Publishers, 1983. pp. 110–19.

BAINTON, Roland H. *Hunted Heretic: The Life and Death of Michael Servetus, 1511–1553.* Boston: Beacon Press, 1953.
———. *Erasmus of Christendom.* London: Collins Fontana, 1969. pp.168–170, 226, 264–65, 275.

GOLDSTONE, Lawrence and Nancy Goldstone. *Out of the Flames: The Story of One of the Rarest Books in the World, and How it Changed the Course of History.* London: Century, 2003.

GORDON, Alexander. "Miguel Serveto-y-Reves," *Theological Review,* vol.LXI: 1878 April; pp.291–92.

[HODGES, Sir Benjamin] *An Impartial History of Michael Servetus, Burnt Alive at Geneva for Heresie.* Aaron Ward, 1724. (Contains Hodges' translation of Lubienjecius' *Historia Reformationis Polonicae,* 1685; Book 2, Chapter 5.)

de MARCOS, Jaume. "Michael Servetus: Martyr to religious freedom," *UU World,* vol.XVII (5): 2003 September/October; p.64.

McKINNEY, Donald W. "The legacy of Miguel Servet," *Kairos,* 1981 Summer/Fall, pp.4–6.

MUTZENBERG, Gabriel. *Michel Servet.* Geneve: La Fondation des Clefs de Saint-Pierre, 1994.

PARKE, David B., editor. *The Epic of Unitarianism: Original Writings from the History of Liberal Religion,* 2d edition. Boston: Skinner House Books, 1985. (Extracts from Servetus's *On the Errors of the Trinity, pp.2–6.*)

PETTEGREE, Andrew. "Michael Servetus and the limits of tolerance," *History Today,* 1990 February, pp.40–45.

Seeing Geneva [running title of an unidentified guide book], pp.40-41.

SERVETUS, Michael. *Christianismi Restitutio,* 1553. (Translated extracts as published in *Christian Life,* 1878 October–December and 1926 January.)

WENDEL, François. *Calvin: The Origins and Development of his Religious Thought.* Translated by Philip Mairet. London: Collins Fontana, 1963 pp.53–55, 93–98.

WILBUR, Earl Morse. *A History of Unitarianism:* [vol.1] *Socinianism and its Antecedents.* Cambridge, MA: Harvard University Press, 1947. Chapters 5, 9–16.
———. "Servetus's ordeal—seen 400 years later," 1953.

A Martyr Soul Remembered:
Commemorating the 450th Anniversary of the
Death of Michael Servetus

DAY II

Saturday, 25th October 2003

— ~ —

MORNING: Centre International Reformé
John Knox

EARLY AFTERNOON: Free time

LATE AFTERNOON: Centre International Reformé
John Knox

EVENING: Personal reflections

A Martyr Soul Remembered

2

THE INFLUENCE OF MICHAEL SERVETUS ON DÁVID FERENCZ (FRANCIS DÁVID) AND THE BEGINNINGS OF TRANSYLVANIAN UNITARIANISM

Rezi Elek*
Deputy Bishop, Transylvanian Unitarian Church and
Dean, Unitarian Theological Faculty,
Protestant Seminary, Koloszvar

— ~ —

Introduction

Today, I would like to express my gratitude for Michael Servetus's spiritual influence on Dávid Ferencz (Francis Dávid) and Transylvanian Unitarianism. This honor is due to the fact—which has not been emphasized so far—that Dávid Ferencz was the most important Hungarian spokesperson for

* Editor's note: Hungarian usage places the given name(s) after the family name. This practice is followed here in the case of Hungarian names, including the author's. Transylvania's Unitarians speak Hungarian.

the theological ideas of Michael Servetus in the middle part of 16th century.

The Servetus heritage—which had apparently been judged on 27 October 1553, here in Geneva— made Transylvanian Unitarianism fruitful, in spite of the social, economic and political situation of that time.

Let me take you on a spiritual journey: Michael Servetus and Dávid Ferencz were born in almost the same year. Servetus in 1511, Dávid in 1510 (only the later researches mention 1520). What would the spiritual exchanges between them have been, if they had met personally? If Servetus had come to Koloszvar, instead of Geneva? Those personal meetings and discussions remain a wonderful exercise of the imagination, but we can follow their spiritual legacy by reading their books, and we are inheritors of this legacy. This is why I would like to express my deep respect for the great Spanish (and may I say, European) thinker on behalf of Transylvanian Unitarianism.

I would like to dispute firmly Jerome Friedman's statement, that Servetus's ideas had little influence on Transylvanian Unitarianism. It might be that Friedman did not know Dávid's works well. I believe that for general information he should have come to Transylvania before publishing his work in 1978. Due to the lack of original sources his conclusions are, in the final analysis, contradicted by the facts. He does not pay attention to the mutual influence, which existed between the antitrinitarian thinkers and movements in 16th century.

This was a special current of the Radical Reformation, and a struggle we know very well from the work of the great scholar George Huntson Williams. Friedman's statement is also contradicted by Balázs Mihály, who is an outstanding current Hungarian historian of Antitrinitarianism. But the influence of Servetus's theology on Dávid's theology was mentioned even during the first half of 20th century by our Unitarian theologian Borbély István.

Preliminaries

In Transylvanian theological history there have been two opinions regarding Servetus's influence on Dávid's theological development:

- The representatives of the first opinion deny Servetus's influence on Dávid's theology. This includes people such as Jakab Elek, historian, and Erdõ János, church historian.

Their conclusion is based on Dávid's declaration,

> My God is my witness that the things which I have learnt, which I have thought and which I still teach, came not from the Koran, or the Talmud, or Servetus, but

from the word of the living God. I am
sure that I am on the way of truth, and
guided by laws of truth. I rest all my
explanation on what is contained in
Scripture.

Their main argument was Dávid's faithfulness to
the Bible: that in the Bible Dávid found his main
theological view, "God is One!", and thus his
theological view is independent, without any
influence from Servetus or others. They referred to
Dávid's famous conclusion,

There is no other clearer and more
evident teaching in the Scripture than the
teaching of God's unity, because the
Scripture asserts that God is the Father
of Jesus Christ and Creator of all things.

- The second opinion was held by those who assert
  and emphasize Servetus's influence on Dávid
  Ferencz, such as Borbély István, and Balázs
  Mihály.

They argue that in some parts of Dávid's work
one can find, in almost the same places, the same text
as in Servetus's work—proving that Dávid adopted
the theological standpoint of Servetus.

My Assessment
For the sake of objectivity I start my review with
a remark of Dávid,

After the events concerning Erasmus in
Rotterdam, how much misery,
humiliation was suffered by Michael
Servetus, who was a great scholar and a
humble servant of God and a truth-seeker.
He, whose works show the errors of false
teachers, was burned [to death] in Geneva
by those who misunderstood his true
religion.

It is incontestable that Dávid not only knew of,
but thoroughly studied Servetus's major works, and
sympathized particularly with the ideas of
Christianismi Restitutio. If we make a comparative
study between Dávid's work, *De Regno Christi liber
primus, De Regno Antichristi liber secundus,* with
Servetus's work, *Christianismi Restitutio,* we can
easily recognize the similarities.

Borbély István compared the two books and
proved that Dávid took over 40% from Servetus's
book. These similarities, according to Borbély, mean
that in 1569 Dávid accepted fully half of Servetus's
thought as part of his own theological thinking.
Moreover, in 1981, other literary historians, such as
Spielman József and Deé Nagy Anikó, asserted that
according to a comparison of the two books only 10–
15 pages are without very strong similarities. And
they considered that the *De Regno Christi*...was in
fact a partially edited version of the *Christianismi
Restitutio.*

In my opinion, the statistical comparison does not mean that Dávid adopted Servetus's theological thinking uncritically. During the turbulence of the Transylvanian reformation, with its famous disputes and political changes, Dávid steeled himself with antitrinitarian ideas, declaring firmly,

> My enemies can write, speak against my conviction, because I know in whom I believe [One God], and I cannot keep this truth secret, but must try to tell it out, while my God gives me spiritual strength for writing and speaking.

I consider that, based upon the examination above, in addition to these two opinions, we should assert a third opinion, as regards Servetus's influence on Dávid Ferencz.

- To my mind Servetus's theological view motivated Dávid to continue on his Reformation path. We cannot speak of simply adoption, but of re-evaluation. Servetus helped Dávid clarify his original theological system. Thus Dávid—like other reformers—did not simply replicate Servetus's work, but developed his ideas independently.

We can prove this independent struggle if we compare Dávid's and Servetus's theological thinking:

1. Biblical proofs

Dávid's intention was to eliminate from Servetus's work all philosophical arguments (Plato's philosophy). He tried to return entirely to the Bible, avoiding all metaphysical proofs, because his conviction was that the doctrine of the Trinity cannot be proved from the Bible. And this is right! (*See*: Anthony F. Buzzard and Charles F. Hunting, *The Doctrine of Trinity. Christianity's Self-Inflicted Wound,* 1998.)

2. Christology

It is well known that traditional Christian theology maintains the pre-existence of Christ, but could not give an adequate answer to the simple question: What was Christ doing from the Creation until time that the Virgin Mary gave birth to him?

It is interesting that one of the greatest 16th-century Hungarian Calvinist theologians, Gelei Katona István, could not answer the question and said that this is, "...[the] Secret of secrets, which must be believed without any explanation...." Servetus, who believed in Christ's pre-existence, could not answer the question entirely either, but he emphasized the importance of the role of the historical Jesus, "This historical Jesus," Servetus said, "was born for us. Moreover you must believe that He was born for you personally."

Dávid adopted Servetus's teaching on the historical Jesus but denied Jesus' pre-existence, and thus he thought that he had answered the question correctly. Dávid asserted, "Christ, the Son of God did not exist at the beginning of the Creation, but only from the time when He was born from Mary." Dávid even declared that those who teach the pre-existence of Christ are Anti-Christ.

3. Old and New Testaments

The differing views of Christological doctrine led to differing evaluations of the Old and New Testaments. According to Dávid, the New Testament is much more valuable than the Old Testament, because Jesus Christ is revealed in the New Testament. Servetus's conviction that the Old Testament points to Christ was not accepted by Dávid.

4. Holy Spirit

There were various theological interpretations of the doctrine of the Holy Spirit in those days. Calvin accepted the divinity and thus adoration of the Holy Spirit. Servetus accepted the divinity of the Holy Spirit, but not his adoration. Dávid rejected both the divinity (as a person of the Trinity) and adoration of the Holy Spirit. He said, "The Holy Spirit is God himself with his power."

5. Baptism

According to church historians, the best common link between Servetus's and Dávid's theological interpretations was the interpretation of baptism. Servetus argued against infant baptism, claiming that before receiving baptism one needs faith. Dávid and his followers accepted it uncritically, but in typical Transylvanian circumstances they could not accept what Servetus taught theologically about the essence of baptism, "that this is a special union with Christ's heavenly body."

They considered that this view went farther even than the Anabaptists' conception, and in Transylvanian circumstances they did not want to be accused by the 'enemies'—particularly Calvinists— that they were propagating Anabaptist ideas. That is why they omitted the whole chapter on baptism from Servetus's book (*De Baptisma Officiae*). However, they did accept adult baptism at age 30, following the model of Jesus.

It is interesting from the point of view of the history of dogma, that Dávid and his followers used the traditional Christian baptismal formula, found in Matthew 28:19, but emphasized that using this formula did not mean that they baptized in the name of the Trinity. They considered the baptismal formula to be simply a confession about the Father, the Son and the Holy Spirit. In the last pages of Servetus's work *De Ordine Mysterium Regenerationis (On the*

Order of Renewal of Sacraments), there are 20 *ratio* (arguments) against paedobaptism, and 25 *vero discriptio* for the real baptism, adult baptism. Dávid adopted these arguments entirely but re-evaluated them.

This short comparative theological review conclusively proves how much Dávid appreciated Servetus's theological thinking and how he re-evaluated it.

~

Christianismi Restitutio and Transylvania

It is very well known that Servetus's major work was burned with him at the stake. The Church authorities in Geneva and the Jesuits in France, who had intended to try Servetus in Vienne, attempted to find and destroy the remaining copies. This work accomplished its purpose: Today from the thousand original copies only three survive, in Paris, Edinburgh, and Vienna. The fourth original copy, last known to be in Kassel, disappeared without a trace during the first half of 18th century.

Obviously, the interesting question is: How did Dávid obtain a copy of *Christianismi Restitutio* in such extreme circumstances? Dávid obtained not an original, but a copy which had been taken into Transylvania by the antitrinitarian thinker Georgio Blandrata (c.1515–1590), who was at that time the court doctor to Transylvania's ruler János Zsigmond.

It is supposed that Blandrata found this copy in Zurich or in Basel, when he had resided there in 1557. He introduced Servetus's book into Transylvania in 1563, of course secretly. Unfortunately we do not know what happened to this copy; presumably it was destroyed after Dávid's trial by 'his enemies.'

I would like to call your attention to a special Transylvanian interest in Servetus's work, which is also an interesting part of European cultural history.

A Transylvanian Unitarian, Szentiványi Márkos Dániel, travelling in England discovered an original *Christianismi Restitutio* in London and immediately bought it on the 13th May 1665. Szentiványi brought this rare and valuable copy with him to Transylvania; this is the copy now in Vienna. This copy later provided Cristoph De Murr (1753–1811) , the famous 18th-century German bibliophile, the opportunity to reprint *Christianismi Restitutio*. How could the German bibliophile have obtained this valuable copy? The answer was found in the last decade's archival research. I will tell you the story of what happened.

According to the note of ownership, the first owner of the original copy was Szentiványi Márkos Dániel, who bought the book in London in 1665. Subsequently, he was Unitarian bishop from 1684 to 1689. The next owner, according to the note of ownership, was Almási Gergely Mihaly, who was also Unitarian bishop—from 1692 to 1794. The note states that the proprietary rights belong to the current bishop, but the succeeding bishops, Pálffy Zsigmond (1724–1737), Szentábrahámi Lombárd Mihály (1737–1758) and Agh István (1758–1737), did not have notes of ownership for this document.

Gál Kelemen, Unitarian church historian, explained this lack of the note of ownership by saying that Servetus's work was owned by the Unitarian bishop, but had to be kept secretly. Gál asserts, "We should not talk in terms of the property rights of the bishop, but rather about the protection of a spiritual heritage."

The carefully kept book entered into the possession of the firmly Calvinist bibliophile, Count Teleki Samuel, in 1780. Even today we do not know exactly how and why this valuable book entered into Teleki's possession, or why Bishop Agh Istvan (or maybe Lázár Istvan) gave up its safekeeping. According to Unitarian church historians, Bishop Agh presented the book to Teleki in 1780 because, at that time, Transylvanian Unitarians were being severely oppressed and Teleki had influence in the Catholic court of Vienna. Interestingly, one year later—in 1781—Emperor Joseph II declared an Edict of Toleration which guaranteed some rights for Protestants in the Hapsburg Empire.

The German bibliophile De Murr, somehow heard that the book was in Teleki's possession and tried to obtain it for reprinting. He bombarded Teleki with letters asking him to sell it to him or to make a copy for his Library. Teleki kept the original but promised De Murr that he would make a copy and send it to him.

Teleki, in a letter, dated 28 August 1785, informed De Murr that, "Servetus's book is near me, and the work for a certified copy starts under my protection." Then in his letter of 20 January 1786, Teleki informed De Murr that, "the copy is ready and I passed it with my official seal to an agent," who would send it from Vienna to the German bibliophile. Teleki was very careful. He made two duplicate copies, one for De Murr and one for himself.

Four years later, in 1790, De Murr used Teleki's copy to print the *Christianismi Restitutio* in Nürnberg with quite a wide circulation despite the disapproval of church officials. Today it is clear that De Murr's main purpose was not to enlarge his library but to reprint Servetus's work. The exchange between Teleki and De Murr after the reprint of Servetus's book is very meaningful. De Murr, in one of his letters addressed to Teleki, wrote, "I appreciate this man (Servetus) as much as I shudder from the evil-minded Calvin's attitude."

Teleki, in his reply of 20 January 1786, wrote that Servetus was a 'non-integrated mind' and tried to justify Calvin's attitude. Teleki later donated the original copy to the Emperor Joseph II (this is the Vienna copy), but he kept one copy for himself, which is today in the Teleki Library in Maros-Vasarhely. This copy was compared with De Murr's copy—today in Harvard University Library—and it is clear that copier is the same person, namely Vitéz József. So, that is how Szentiványi and Transylvanian Unitarians contributed to the maintenance of Servetus's spiritual legacy.

~

Conclusion

Finally, I would like to call your attention to an interesting occurrence of the anti-Servetian struggle immediately after his death. The students who entered the Theological School in Geneva had to sign a Confession-formula before the Rector. This Confession had been formulated by Calvin himself, and it required a devoted attitude and humble obedience to Calvin's doctrines. Whoever did not sign could not become a student of the School. It is noteworthy that in the Confession-formula there is a statement damning Servetus's teaching. "I damn all the heresies, which the First Nicean, the Effezian and the Calcedonian Synods damned, with the heresy that Servetus and his henchman renewed."

I would like to conclude my paper with Henrik Tollin's thought, "'My era', says Servetus, 'despised me. I lived for the next generation. Do you understand what I wanted and why I died?'"

Dávid Ferencz and his followers in Transylvania understood what he wanted and why he died. Today, in 2003 at the memorial of the 450th anniversary of his death, I am sure that all who are here understand what he wanted and why he died. This understanding is an impulse in all of us for freedom and the search for truth.

~

SOURCES

BAINTON, Roland H. *Hunted Heretic. The Life and Death of Michael Servetus (1511–1553).* Boston, 1953.

BALÁZS Mihály. Az erdélyi antitrinitárizmus az 1560-as évek végén. Akadémiai kk.Bp. 1988.

BORBÉLY István. A magyar unitárius egyház hitelvei a XVI.században. Forrástanulmány. Koloszvár, 1914.
————. A mai unitárius hitelvek kialakulásának története. Cluj-Kvár, 1925.
————. Melyik évben kezdődött az unitárizmus Erdélyben? Erdélyi Múzeum XXXVI. 1931. pp.224–39.

BUZZARD, F. Anthony, and HUNTING, F. Charles. *The Doctrine of the Trinity. Christianity's Self-Inflicted Wound.* Lanham-New York-Oxford: International Scholar Publication, 1998.

DÁVID Ferencz. Rovid Magyarazatat mikeppen az Anthichrisztus, az Igaz istenrõl valo tudomant meg homalioitotta. Albae Iuliae. Anno Christi M.D.LXVII. (RMNy 232). Rövid Magyarázat. Az eredeti kiadás fakszimiléjével. Koloszvár, 1910.

————. Rövid útmutatás az Istennek ígéjének igaz értelmére, mostani szentháromságról támadott vetélkedésének megfejtésére és itéletére hasznos és szükséges. Albae Iuliae, 1567. (Modern kiadása: Németh S.Katalin által. Bp. 1984.)

————. *De falsa et vera unius Dei patri....* Alba Iuliae, 1568. (Vö.B.M. 242)

————. *De regno Christis liber primus. De regno Antichristi liber secundus. Acessit tractatus de circumcissione.* Alba Iuliae, 1569.

ERDÕ János. Teológiai tanulmányok. Koloszvár, 1986.

————. *Transylvanian Unitarian Church. Chronological and Theological Essays.* Translated by GELLÉRD Judit. The Center for Free Religion. Chico. 1990.

FRIEDMAN, Jerome. *Michael Servetus. A Case Study in Total Heresy.* Genéve 1978. (BM.70)

GÁL Kelemen. A kolozsvári unitárius kollégium története. (Kvár). 1935. II. kötet. (403)

GAVRUCZA Emese. Kálvin-hitvallás a

beirítkozáskor. Református Szemle. 2002. 6.szám. 519.

GELLÉRD Imre. Dávid Ferencz munkái Vö

GORDON Sándor. Angliai levelezés. KM XXV (1890). 266.

JAKAB Elek. Dávid Ferencz emléke. Bp. 1879.

KANYRÓ Ferencz. Servét miért akart 1553-ban Nápolyba menekülni? Uo. XXXVII.237.
————. Servét életrajzához észrevétel. Uo. XIII.123.
————. Servét-pör. Uo. XLVI.55.
————. Unitáriusok Magyarországon.tekintettel az unitárizmus általános történetére. Kvár, 1891.

KISS Áron. A XVI.szátadban tartott magyar református zsinatok végzései. Bp. 1882.

LAMPE, Friedrich Adolf and EMBER Pál Debreczeni. *Historia Ecclesiae Reformatae in Hungaria et Transylvania.* Utrecht, 1728. (BM.243)

SERVET, Miquel. *De Trinitatis Erroribus Libri Septem.* Per Michaelm Serveto, alias Reuses ab Aragonia Hispanum. Anno MDXXXI. (Fakszimile kiadása: Frankfurt a.M. 1965)
————. *Christianismi Restitutio.* Vienne 1553. (Fakszimile kiadása: Frankfurt a.M. 1966)

A hit Isten ajándéka.1568–1993. Kvár. Innen: SIMÉN Domokos. János Zsigmond valláspolitikája. 12.

SIMÉN Domokos. Szervét Mihály jellemrajzához észrevétel. KerMagv XIII( ). 123.

SPIELMAN József, SEBESTYÉN Mihály, and DEÉ Nagy Anna. Miquel Servetus műve és Erdély. In. Korunk XL. 1981. 559-602. (BM.248)

Szervét könyve. Unitárius Élet. 1976.2.szám. 7.

TOLLIN, Henrik. Szervét Mihály jellemrajza. Ford. Simén Domokos. KerMagv XIII.1.

WILBUR, Earl Morse. *A History of Unitarianism in Transylvania, England and America.* Cambridge, 1962.

WILLIAMS, George Huntston. *The Radical Reformation.* Philadelphia, 1962.

3

WHY UNITARIANS AND UNIVERSALISTS OWE MORE TO JOHN CALVIN THAN THEY DO TO MICHAEL SERVETUS

Andrew M. Hill
Minister, St. Mark's Unitarian Church,
Edinburgh, Scotland

— ~ —

Part of my childhood was spent across the River Mersey from Liverpool. There, in a glass-topped show case in Wallasey's beautiful art-nouveau Unitarian church was a very old English language Bible: a *Geneva Bible,* translated and first published here, in Geneva, by British Protestant exiles from Queen Mary Tudor's restored Catholicism. One of those exiles was the Scottish reformer John Knox for whom this centre is named, and who made it abundantly clear in 'a monstrous blast' against Anabaptists what he would have thought about our gathering here on this anniversary:

> Servetus [wrote Knox] was an
> abominable blasphemer against God and

you are justifiers of Servetus; therefore ye
are blasphemers before God, like
abominable as he was.

I doubt Knox's distaste for Servetus and his
justifiers would be mollified, even if he knew that I'm
about to suggest that Unitarians and Unitarian
Universalists actually owe less to Servetus and more
to his friend and mentor John Calvin; a suggestion,
highly provocative among Unitarians and Unitarian
Universalists at the best of times, but on this
occasion, probably treason!

But before coming to that, I want to say what I'm
not saying, and then mention one or two things about
how we do Unitarian, Universalist and Unitarian-
Universalist history.

Straight away then, I'm not making any apology
for Calvin's part in the death of Servetus. It was a
barbaric act which I wouldn't defend even on the
grounds that it was typical 16th century barbarism.
Nor, would I suggest that the case of Michael
Servetus was insignificant in the struggle for religious
liberty. So straightway I affirm with Castellio, "To
kill a man is not to defend a doctrine; it is to kill a
man."

On the other hand, sensing an impending
apocalypse, Servetus was no shining example of
gentleness calling Calvin a, "worthless and shameless

twister!" Nor would I doubt that Servetus was a true Renaissance person versed in ancient and modern languages, and living on the frontiers of 16th-century medicine, science, astronomy and geography although, as far as the Scots were concerned, he was clearly ill-informed, "Their temper [he wrote] is hasty, prone to revenge, and fierce. . .Unfriendly in disposition, [the Scots] look down on all other mortals."

Nor do I want to imply that Servetus's speculations about the Trinity, his trial and cruel death were not catalysts for wide-spread speculation. But some scholars do point out that Servetus's anti-trinitarianism was rather different from that of Dávid, Socinus and the later Unitarians. Jerome Friedman, for example, summarises the differences thus:

> His system had no room for an adoptionism predicated upon a human Jesus Christ who was unable to deify man since he himself was not divine. Consequently, where Unitarianism unified the Godhead by depriving it of Christ, Servetus unified the Godhead by divesting Christ of his humanity and by subordinating the remaining divine existence to the Father.

And therefore, according to Friedman, Servetus was not a Unitarian.

Now, about how we do Unitarian and Unitarian-Universalist history, two things. Firstly, there is a difference between the history of Unitarian ideas, and the history of Unitarian people—they aren't always the same. Jeremy Goring describes the Unitarian ideas school, "...as some kind of benevolent infection that broke out in eastern Europe in the 16th century and later spread to England and America."

His prime example is Wilbur's *History of Unitarianism*, several chapters of the first volume of which are devoted to Servetus as a prime source of this infection. Of course, there is a Unitarian story here, but it flits and jumps and only sometimes, as in Transylvania, becomes a story of 'Unitarian people.' When Wilbur gets to Britain and America, he tells the stories of many early congregations, "before they became properly Unitarian" in about four pages for America and two for Britain, dismissing their stories as, "...apart from the main current of the stream of history that we are following."

But it is exactly this early history, "before they became properly Unitarian," which laid down for us the foundations of our religious style, the manner of our worship and how we organise ourselves.

And secondly, about how we do our history, because there is so much of it, we inevitably and unavoidably do it in convenient and disjointed parts:

- either just our own country's Unitarian history;
- or the stories of significant individuals—
  Servetus, Dávid, Priestley and Emerson for
  example;
- or the stories of particular tributaries—an
  Anabaptist tributary, for example, in Poland and
  a General Baptist one in England, or the
  Universalist tributary (in America, really
  another mainstream); or the transcendentalist,
  humanist, feminist and pagan tributaries on the
  main-stream's English-speaking bank.

These are all good stories and they have all
contributed lots and lots of energy to the mainstream,
but they are not the mainstream. So where does the
Unitarian mainstream flow from and from whence
does it spring? Let's eliminate some possibilities.

Does it spring from Catholic Christianity?

A few Unitarian groups have come directly from
Catholic Christian sources. Deutsche Katholicismus
in the 1840s was later absorbed in the German Free
Religious movement. Both Iglesia Filipina Indepen-
diente at the start of the 20th century and The
Czechoslovak Church in the 1920s flowed in a
Unitarian direction for a while and then veered back
towards Christian orthodoxy. Norbert Čapek, founder
of The Religious Society of Czech Unitarians, was
born a Catholic but came to Unitarianism as a Baptist.
Presently The Unitarian Universalist Church of the
Philippines and fledgling Spanish-speaking groups in

Spain, South and Central America and within the
Unitarian Universalist Association belong to the
international Unitarian and Universalist movement,
but these are recent small Catholic tributaries to the
mainstream.

Anglican (or Episcopalian) Christianity has
always been troubled with Unitarian tendencies—and
still is. Wilbur devotes two whole chapters to them;
and Anglican seceders like Theophilus Lindsey in
England have influenced the Unitarian mainstream;
but only one Anglican church, King's Chapel Boston,
has ever transferred from Anglicanism to Unitarianism and that was in exceptional circumstances which
have never been repeated.

What about Lutheran Christianity?

Lutheranism led the way in Transylvania. Dávid
was, at one time, a Lutheran bishop, but in the
controversy over the real presence of Christ in the
Lord's Supper, the Hungarians embraced Calvinism.
Lutheran pietism influenced George de Benneville
and early Universalism. There have been isolated
break-away German free-thought congregations and
today's German Unitarians have their roots there, but
the only seceding Lutheran congregations have been
the Icelandic and Norwegian Unitarian churches of
the North American prairies.

So of the main historic divisions of the Christian
church, that leaves the Reformed Protestant Chris-

tianity, which springs and flows from the Swiss Reformation, and in particular from the ecclesiastical reforms associated with Geneva and its pivotal figure John Calvin; and it is this that I would identify as the spring from which flows the Unitarian mainstream.

The debt of Unitarians to the Reformed tradition of Protestant Christianity is, perhaps, most obvious when you look at the Unitarian churches of Poland and Transylvania. Both derived from divisions within Reformed Protestant Christian synods. In Transylvania, even today, from outward appearances it is quite hard to distinguish heterodox and orthodox varieties of Reformed Protestant Christianity. Both varieties of ministers wear black gowns, both varieties have consistories or synods where ministers and laity share power, and both elect superintendents whom they call "bishops". Had the Minor Reformed Church in Poland survived as an organised Unitarian church, these things would probably be true there as well.

In England and Wales and America, it's rather more complicated because the English church reformation was only partial, and doctrinal development towards Unitarianism came much later. Those who wanted further reforms along the Genevan model—the so-called Puritans—either using a synodical or an independent parish model, were obliged to continue agitating.

Some first generation Puritans, tired of agitating, emigrated to America where they set up in New England, 'a godly Commonwealth,' along Genevan lines, with a standing order of independent town churches established by law. America's oldest Unitarian churches belonged to the Massachusetts Standing Order as defined by *The Cambridge Platform* of 1648.

In 'old' England, another generation of English Puritans continued agitating for Genevan type reforms from within the Church of England. Their high point came during the English Civil War, when Parliament called an assembly to advance church reform. Its lasting monument is *The Westminster Confession of Faith*, English-speaking Calvinism's classic code of doctrine. But the English republic turned sour. The British monarchy was restored, episcopacy in England and Wales was revived; and 'two thousand' Puritan clergy were 'ejected' from the Church of England and obliged to attempt Genevan-style reforms in circumstances as inhospitable as those of their American cousins were hospitable. But around some of these ejected Puritan ministers, congregated churches of reluctant dissenters, which a century later transformed into British Unitarian congregations.

Thus the mainstream of the Unitarian movements of Poland, Transylvania, Britain and America can be traced back to a Genevan source, the Swiss Reformation and the Reformed Protestant stream of Christianity; and organised Unitarian movements have inherited many of its characteristics.

The most significant characteristic of the Swiss Reformation was its restoration of the Word of God as central to worship. Even today when, as Frederick Hosmer says in one of his hymns, "the Word moves on" to include poetry, music, art and dance, Unitarian and Unitarian Universalist practice continues to reflect a preaching rather than a sacramental heritage.

Preaching's centrality is also seen in how Unitarians worship—a style developed from the liturgy of the Word which opened the Catholic Mass—although in England the different, but approximate pattern, of Anglican Morning and Evening Prayer was also involved. Even our hymn books were originally expanded metrical Psalters: the Psalms, as biblical songs, being the only vocals the Genevan reformers allowed, the most famous example being "The Old Hundredth".

Again, the importance of preaching-centred worship is reflected in the architecture of older Unitarian churches and meeting houses. Reformed re-ordering of pre-Reformation churches—westward pulpit-facing seats in the shorter architectural 'choir' facing eastward pulpit-facing seats in the longer nave—was amazingly still reflected when Koloszvar's Unitarian Church was built more than two hundred years later! Elsewhere, the architectural 'choir' shrivelled completely, pulpit and seating being arranged for the best hearing of the Word, and the table diminished in prominence or brought out only as needed. A clear line of development links the often beautifully austere and carefully decorated early churches and meeting houses of Transylvania, old and new England and Ireland with Frank Lloyd Wright's stunningly modernist Unitarian and Universalist churches of Wisconsin and Oak Park, Illinois, in America.

Another characteristic of Reformed Protestant Christianity was its understanding of 'the church'; not 'the church' as separated out from society as with many Anabaptists, but 'the church' as co-extensive with society. As the civil power has public responsibility for the welfare of human bodies, so the church has public responsibility for the welfare of human souls; and even when Unitarians have found themselves in non-establishment and dissenting circumstances, the mind-set of public responsibility has come with them. I'll identify three ways:

- Firstly, this public mind-set is the source the deep seated Unitarian desire for a comprehensive, all-embracing church as when Channing declared, "We must shun the spirit of sectarianism as from hell." Only the Bible and the Divine Unity were common enough to embrace all Christians, said the Unitarians;

and later it was even claimed that the Divine Unity was a sufficient basis for all faiths.

- Secondly, the notion that church and state serve the same constituency explains why Unitarians regard their ordinances as available publicly to all, not just privately for the 'saved'. In New England, a major factor in the emergence of Unitarian parishes was the orthodox effort to rescind this heritage and confine ordinances to church members alone.

As to practice, Unitarians have followed the Reformed pattern of the Lord's Supper as special and occasional, and in English-speaking lands, where Unitarian emergence and anti-sacramentalism often came together, so 'special and occasional' as often to become 'never'.

Baptism is more complex. A few dispensed with it altogether. Some—Dávid Ferencz, the Racovians, Unitarian General Baptists in England and many American Universalists—influenced either by Anabaptists or by scriptural practice or both, and regarding faith as a matter of adult discretion, reserved baptism for adults. But on the whole, the Unitarian mainstream, while modifying inward understanding according to circumstance, continued according to ancient practice, with some sort of public ceremony, which may or may not involve baptism, following the birth of a child.

A good current example of the Unitarian approach to a special ordinance is marriage. Where other churches have rejected couples as not church members, or as divorced persons, or as of the same sex, Unitarians have put public welfare before private church purity.

- Thirdly, the Reformed view that church and state serve one constituency spurred the extraordinarily fruitful Unitarian contribution to public service, the improvement of human welfare and political involvement [and maybe economic activity]. As well as being about personal faith, religion is also about education, health, social welfare and human liberties; and it is more than interesting that educational opportunity has emerged as a significant factor in the recent business of Transylvanian Unitarians.

As Rezi Elek told the 2001 ICUU Symposium at Oxford:

It is characteristic of the importance Transylvanian Unitarians have attributed to education that the building of a new school has always come before erecting a new church building.

That is good Calvinism!

Yet another aspect of Reformed Protestant Christianity's restoration of 'the Word,' which has been important for Unitarians and Unitarian Universalists, is its use of rediscovered ancient texts, the need to understand them in their original languages, and the endeavour of translating them into spoken tongues. In turn, this gave insights into the language-use of those cultures which nurtured the Hebrew and Christian scriptures and led to the possibility of more accurate Bible translations. This was a renaissance humanist endeavour where Erasmus had led the way for both Catholics and Protestants with his edition of the Greek New Testament which omitted the text, "There are three that bear witness in heaven: the Father, the Word, and the Holy Spirit and these three are one."

Now it was because Reformed Protestant Christianity took textual criticism of the Bible seriously that early Unitarians vigorously claimed Biblical authority for their anti-Trinitarian protests. British Unitarians even had their own *Improved Version of the New Testament.*

But this also meant that there must be a ministry educated in the ancient tongues and places where ancient tongues could be taught. By 1569 the Unitarians had taken over the Reformed school in Koloszvar. Racow's famous, but short-lived, Academy was founded in 1602. Harvard College was established at Cambridge, Massachusetts, in 1638 exactly for the purpose of educating ministers; and after 1689 Dissenters barred from English universities set up their own academies on the Genevan model. Harris Manchester College at Oxford, where ICUU held its 2001 Symposium, is the descendent of one such dissenting academy; and it was James Martineau, its sometime principal who wrote, "… reason is the ultimate appeal, the supreme tribunal, to the test of which even Scripture must be brought."

Thus the Unitarian respect for the rational human intellect, for the textual and form criticism of ancient sacred texts, for an educated ministry and for education in general can be traced back directly to the Academy which John Calvin established at Geneva and where he placed the unfortunate Castellio in charge.

I must turn now to theology, because contrary to popular opinion the doctrine of double predestination was not the keystone of John Calvin's theology. That's a distortion of his successors. For Calvin the keystone was, "everything—including predestination—to the glory of God." But, more importantly, the corollary of 'all to the glory of God' was Calvin's doctrine of human total depravity and its consequence—the complete inability of human persons to help themselves. In the years following Calvin this produced knock-on effects:

- First, a Dutch Reformed pastor, Jacobus

Arminius, protested that grace was resistible and could be earned, and so people "could work out their own salvation." Similar protests occurred in the British Isles and in North America.

- Secondly, these Arminian protests were countered by a new insistence on subscription to the detail of Reformed Protestant Confessions of Faith; and

- Thirdly, this new insistence on doctrinal subscription produced its own reaction with the emergence within Reformed Protestant Christianity of non-subscribing parties.

The earliest non-subscribing party was the Dutch Remonstrant Brotherhood in 1619, followed a century later by the Salters' Hall controversy which divided English dissenters, and in 1725 both the reorganising of Irish non-subscribing ministers into their own presbytery, and the abolition of subscription here in Geneva. In fact, The Encyclopaedists went so far as to call Geneva "a Socinian city". Despite the best efforts of Le Réveil (The Awakening) in the early 19th century and of the crisis theologies in the 20th, these liberalising currents continue running within the Reformed Protestant Christian churches of Europe. But Unitarians and Unitarian Universalists seem to have largely lost touch with them.

But also, in the embryology of the English-speaking Unitarianism of northern Europe and America, the Arminian protest against the Calvinist view of depraved human nature turns out to be far more significant than any protest against the Trinitarian God. Trinitarianism lost its significance, not so much because it is theologically questionable, but more because Trinitarian language is largely unscriptural and scripture takes precedent over confessions of faith. "The Bible has it by four!" was the cry of the non-subscribing majority at the Salters' Hall meeting in London; whereas in southern Europe—where the Trinity was a crunch issue for converting Jews and Moors in Spain, hence Servetus's interest—and in Transylvania, where the Muslim Ottomans were continually knocking on the door, the Trinitarian nature of God was far more significant.

A new wave of English-speaking Unitarians and Universalists, found themselves responding to the hyper-Calvinism of the Revivalists. James Relly, formerly a follower of George Whitfield, claimed that if all had sinned in Adam, then all were automatically saved in Christ. John Murray agreed with him and went to America to say so; and Joseph Priestley, the English Unitarian raised a Calvinist, simply moved the goal posts so that, eventually, everyone was predestined for heaven. With this, Priestley was one with the American Universalist Elhanan Winchester. A recent American author, Ann Lee Bressler, has succinctly called this 'Calvinism Improved.'

But the reluctant Unitarian, William Ellery Channing, regarded Priestley's and the Universalists' response as cold, calculating and mechanical. For him, the real problem with Calvinism was that it was utterly immoral and contradicted, "our best ideas of goodness and justice":

> We believe that God is infinitely good, kind, benevolent, in the proper sense of these words [he said in his 1819 propaganda sermon *Unitarian Christianity*]; good in disposition, as well as in act; good, not to a few, but to all; good to every individual, as well as to the general system.

Now 'Channing Unitarianism' spread like wildfire across America, Britain and Europe. Channing's collected works were published in Britain in 1843, in France by mid-century, in Germany in 1850 and in Hungarian between 1870 and 1881. Also it was a Channing tract which brought Hajom Kissor Singh and the Khasi Unitarians out of dark Welsh Calvinism into Unitarian light. But note, that it was not so much his Unitarianism which was the magic of Channing, but his recovered understanding of, "the inherent worth and dignity of every person".

Hugh Trevor-Roper has pointed out that Calvinism is 'an obscurantist deviation' from a wider

and broader Arminian–Socinian river which has, "a
distinct origin, a continuous tradition, and a pedigree
longer than Calvinism."

Indeed so, but so far as the organised Unitarian
and Universalist movements of Europe, North
America, Asia and the Antipodes are concerned, the
corrections to this deviation have mostly occurred
within a heritage and a culture re-moulded and re-
constructed out of medieval Catholicism by the
Protestant Reformers of Geneva. And even if we have
long ago divorced ourselves from the worst effects of
Calvin's theology, its replacements remain, and many
other characteristics of this heritage are very much in
place.

Here then, in conclusion, is a brief balance sheet
of what Unitarians and Universalists have acquired
from Servetus and what they have acquired from the
Reformed Protestant Christianity with which Calvin
was associated. From Servetus we have inherited:

- a catalyst for speculation upon the natures and
  relationships of God as Trinity;
- a necessary horror at the manner and cruelty of
  his death leading to a passion for religious
  tolerance and the free exercise of religious faith;
- a splendid story about a complex, very
  impatient Renaissance man with wide medical,
  scientific and theological knowledge;
- three UUA societies and a very dissonant hymn

tune in *Singing the Living Tradition* named for him.

On the other hand from John Calvin and the tradition of Reformed Protestant Christianity, Unitarians and Unitarian Universalists have acquired:

- an antithetical self-help response to the distorted total depravity 'Calvinism' of the Calvinists;
- a non-subscribing 'Bible is sufficient' protest against those who imposed subscription to creeds and confessions of faith;
- a democratic, non-hierarchical style of church polity in the coming together of ministers and lay representatives in synodical or federal assemblies;
- a style of worship and architecture centring on preaching and honouring the critical processes of the human mind; and
- churches, whose members protect its privileges for the benefit of all; maintain a creatively critical relationship between their churches and the civil authorities; and preserve a public mindset envisioning a comprehensive all-embracing church.

As Longfellow penned, "One holy Church of God appears through every age and race, unwasted by the lapse of years, unchanged by changing place."

~

SOURCES

BIBLE. New Testament, Philippians 2: 12; I John 5: 7.

BOLAM, C. G., Jeremy GORING, H. L. SHORT and Roger THOMAS. *The English Presbyterians.* London, 1968. pp.22–25.

BRESSLER, Ann Lee. *The Universalist Movement in America, 1770-1880.* Oxford University Press, 2001. Chapter 1 heading.

BRIGGS, Martin S. *Puritan Architecture and Its Future.* London, 1946.

CHANNING, William Ellery. "Unitarian Christianity," 1928.
———. "The Church," 1841.

CLIFFORD, Sister Mary Dorita. "Iglesia Filipina Indepentiente: the revolutionary church," in Gerald H. Anderson ed., *Studies in Philippine Church History.* Corbell, 1969. pp.223–55.

CROMPTON, Arnold. "Nationalism and a liberal church," *Unitarian Universalist Register-Leader:* 1963 February; pp.11–12.

[FOUR HUNDRED YEARS] 1792–96 'Negyszas Ev 1568–1968. Koloszvar, 1968. p.36.

FRIEDMAN, Jerome. *Michael Servetus: A Case Study in Total Heresy.* Geneva, 1978. p.134.
———. "Michael Servetus: Unitarian, antitrinitarian, or cosmic dualist?" *Proceedings of the Unitarian Universalist Historical Society,* vol. 20(2): 1985–86; pp.10–20.

THE GENEVAN PSALTER. "The Old Hundredth," 1551. The English version is by William Kethe, one of the Genevan community of English exiles from the Marian persecution, and its tune by Louis Bourgeois.

GORDON, Alexander. *Addresses Biographical and Historical.* London, 1922. p.29. Quoted from Servetus's edition of, *Ptolemy's Geography.*

GORING, Jeremy. "Unitarianism: history, myth or make-believe?" *Transactions of the Unitarian Historical Society,* vol.19(4): 1990 April; pp.213–27.

GUDMUNDSON, V. Emil. *The Icelandic Unitarian Connection: Beginnings of Icelandic Unitarianism in North America, 1885–1900.* Winnipeg, 1984.

HENRY, Richard. *Norbert Fabian Capek: A Spiritual Journey.* Boston, 1999.

HILL, Andrew M. "Channing and British Unitarianism: sowing the seeds," *Transactions of the Unitarian Historical Society,* vol.19(2):1988 April; pp.71–77.

———. "William Adam: Unitarian missionary," *Transactions of the Unitarian Historical Society,* vol.21(1):1995 April; pp.30–42.

———. "Unitarier," *Theologische Realenzyklopaedie,* 2002.

———. "James Relly," in *Oxford Dictionary of National Biography,* 2004.

HILL, Andrew M., Jill K. McALLISTER and Clifford M. REED, eds. *A Global Conversation: Unitarian / Universalism at the Dawn of the 21st Century.* Prague: ICUU, 2002. p.63.

HOSMER, F. L. "O Thou in lonely vigil led," *Hymns of Worship Revised,* 1962. No.217.

JONES, Ronald P. *Nonconformist Church Architectture.* London, 1914.

KNOX, John. "An Answer to a great number of blasphemous cavillations written by an Anabaptist and adversarie to God's eternal Predestination" [Geneva, 1560], quoted in I. B. Horst, *The Radical Brethren.* Neiewkoop, 1972. p.119.

KUHN, Annette. "Deutschkatholiken," *Theologische Realenzyklopaedie,* 2002.

LAVAN, Spencer. *Unitarians and India: A Study in Encounter and Response.* Boston, 1977. p.153.

LONG, Arthur J. "Castellio," in H. D. Rack, *The Swiss Connection* (1994), p.63. Quoted by Roland Bainton from, 'Contra Libellum Calvini'.

LONGFELLOW, Samuel. "One holy Church of God appears," *Hymns of the Spirit,* 1864.

MARTINEAU, James. *The Rationale of Religious Inquiry,* 1836.

McLACHLAN, Herbert. *English Education under the Test Acts: Being the History of the Non-conformist Academies 1662–1820.* Manchester, 1931.

MELLONE, S. H. *Liberty and Religion: The First Century of the British and Foreign Unitarian Association.* London, 1925. p.17.

MORGAN, John C. *The Devotional Heart: Pietism and the Renewal of American Unitarian Universalism.* Boston: Skinner House Books, 1995.

MUIR, Frederic John. Maglipay Universalist: A history of the Unitarian Universalist Church of the Philippines, 2001.

NORMAN, Amandus. "Kristofer Janson: As man,

poet and religious reformer," *Proceedings of the Unitarian Historical Society,* vol.2(2):1932; pp.21–40.

OELBERG, Sarah. "Liberal religion on the Norwegian–American frontier." http://www.mankatofellowship.org/nora/tablehi. html

OXFORD DICTIONARY OF THE CHRISTIAN CHURCH, "Geneva Bible." Wallasey's Unitarian Church and its Geneva Bible are now in the care of the Historic Chapels Trust. According to an unidentified press cutting, its Geneva Bible, which now misses its first pages, is dated 1599. ———. "Czechoslovak Church."

PATTERSON, George F. "The rise of Icelandic Churches in America," *Proceedings of the Unitarian Historical Society,* vol.2(2):1932; pp.1–13,14–20.

PAUL, Manfred. "Religious liberalism in Germany," in *Centennial Reflections: International Association for Religious Freedom,* 2001. pp.79–93.

PEASTON, A. Elliott, in *The Prayer Book Reform Movement in the XVIIIth Century* (Oxford, 1940), has traced Anglican influence on Unitarian worship in England.

PETTEGREE, Andrew. *History Today,* 1990 February; p.45a.

PRIESTLEY, Joseph. "Unitarianism explained and defended" (1796), sermon preached in Winchester's Universalist meeting house in Philadelphia.

REES, Thomas. *The Racovian Catechism,* English language version, 1819. A footnote (p.257) gives an interesting description of different Unitarian attitudes to baptism.

RICHARDSON, Robert D., Jr., from, *Emerson:The Mind on Fire.* University of California, 1995. p.291.

RITCHIE, Susan. "The Pasha of Buda and the Edict of Torda: Transylvanian Unitarian / Islamic Ottoman cultural investment," in on-line *Journal of Liberal Religion,* 2003.

ROPER, H. R. Trevor. "The religious origins of the Enlightenment," in *Religion, the Reformation and Social Change and other essays* (1967), p.211. The references to Socinianism at Geneva are in the Encyclopaedia article, "Geneve".

SCOVEL, Carl, and Charles C. FORMAN. *A Journey Towards Independence: King's Chapel's Transition to Unitarianism.* Boston: Skinner House Books, 1993. passim.

Singing the Living Tradition. Boston, 1993. Nos.13 and 302. The tune "Servetus" is 7777D, by Thomas Oboe Lee.

STEERS. David, ed. *European Perspectives on Communion.* Ulster Unitarian Christian Association for the European Liberal Protestant Network, 2001. Contains a series of articles on Unitarian and other Liberal Christian approaches to the Lord's Supper.

THOMAS, Roger. "The non-subscription controversy amongst Dissenters in 1719," *Journal of Ecclesiatical History,* vol.4(2):1953 October; pp.162–86.

WILBUR, E. M. *Our Unitarian Heritage,* 1925 (reprinted 1963), writes, "Servetus was not a Unitarian in any true sense. He was more like a Sabellian," p.62.
———. *A History of Unitarianism,* 2 vols. Cambridge, MA: Harvard University Press.
———. vol.1: *Socinianism and its Antecedents,* 1945. p.359.
———. Chaps. 21–23, "Growth of liberal thought in the Reformed Church in Poland," "Calvinistic reaction in the Reformed Church," "The Minor Reformed Church: early history," pp.294–338.
———. vol.2: *in Transylvania, England and America,* 1952. pp.64, 210.
———. Chap.2, "The early Reformation in

WILBUR, E. M., *cont.*
Transylvania," pp.22–27.
———. Chap.3, "The rise of Unitarianism in Transylvania, 1564–1569," pp.28-43.
———. Chaps.12–13, "The established church in conflict with Socinianism: the Trinitarian controversy;" "The Arian movement in the Church of England," pp. 209–43.

WILLIAMS, George Huntston. *The Radical Reformation* (1962 ed.), says that Servetus was "anti-Nicene" rather than anti-Trinitarian, p.323. Somewhere else he says that he was not "a proper Unitarian".

WORTLEY, F. H. "An inventory of the records of the Particular (Congregational) Churches of Massachusetts gathered 1625–1805," *Harvard Theological Studies,* vol.25:1970; and *Proceedings of the Unitarian Historical Society,* vol.16(1–2):1966–69; p.viii, noted there were 45 17th-century Massachusetts churches which became Unitarian.

WRIGHT, Conrad. *The Beginnings of Unitarianism in America.* Boston, 1954. passim
———. *Congregational Polity: A Historical Survey of Unitarian and Universalist Practice.* Boston, 1997. pp.7–19.

LE MAN

LAC

Tour de
l'Isla

Tour
et
porte

de la
Monnaire

Rivière Rhone

Hospital du Peste

GENEVA AS CALVIN SAW IT

4

SERVETUS AS SACRIFICE

Peter Hughes
Vice President of the
Unitarian Universalist Historical Society

— ~ —

When Theodore Parker visited Geneva in July 1844 he looked for the execution site of Servetus. He himself was in the midst of a struggle with other Boston-area Unitarian ministers who wished to cast him out of the new denomination. After 1841 Parker's colleagues no longer exchanged pulpits with him. Many American Unitarians believed that their own embattled faith would be more defensible if they were not associated with such radicals as Parker. Theirs were the same reasons that had caused Calvin and other reformers to condemn Servetus nearly three hundred years earlier. "At Geneva," said Parker's early biographer, Octavius Brooks Frothingham, "memories of Calvin and Servetus . . . crowd upon him."

Parker later wrote, "Since the days of Seneca and Lucan, perhaps Servetus is [Spain's] foremost man, fantastic minded, yet rich in germs of fertile thought."

He placed Servetus in the class of persons accused of atheism—like Jesus and himself—whom he considered more theistic and religious than their persecutors. Parker included Calvin in a list of pioneers of religious freedom, along with Jesus, Paul, Origen, Pelagius, Hus, Socinus, and Servetus. Calvin, he allowed, was an honest man and astray. "I defy anybody," Parker wrote, "to love Jonathan Edwards's or John Calvin's conception of the Deity .... John Calvin himself," however, "was a great deal better than the Calvinistic idea of God."

In 1853 Parker wrote to Convers Francis, who taught at Harvard, suggesting that he assign students to write graduation papers on Servetus. Parker also observed that for at the recent Unitarian Convention in Worcester, Massachusetts, a delegate had suggested the American Unitarians erect a tricentennial Servetus monument. He recorded that some had objected to this idea, fearing that, "It would offend the orthodox." From this letter it is clear that the spirits of both Michael Servetus and John Calvin were very much alive within the American Unitarians 300 years after the two reformers confronted each other in Geneva.

Parker deemed Calvinism a step forward from earlier forms of Christianity. But he thought religious progress uneven. "Every step in religion is an experiment," he wrote. "If a wrong step it is painful. But the pain is medical." Parker then made a short catalogue of some of the religious disasters in history from which we can benefit. It is interesting to note ancient sacrificial rituals alongside deeds of religious persecution, including an oblique reference to the execution of Servetus. Parker listed,

> The fires of Moloch in Syria; the harsh mutilations in the name of Astarte, Cybele, Jehovah; the barbarities of imperial pagan tormentors; the still grosser torments which Romano-Gothic Christians in Italy and Spain heaped on their brother men, the fiendish cruelties to which Switzerland, France, the Netherlands, England, Scotland, Ireland, America have been witness.

Parker was not alone in likening the death of Servetus to a sacrifice. In 1806 Richard Wright, in his *Apology for Dr. Michael Servetus*, depicted Servetus as a sacrifice and the first martyr for Unitarianism. Other biographers and historians—Robert Willis, Joseph Henry Allen, Stephen Fritchman, Earl Morse Wilbur, John Fulton, and recently Marian Hillar— have stated the contribution of Servetus to liberal religion in sacrificial terms. Hillar wrote, "From a historical perspective, Servetus died in order that freedom of conscience could become a civil right of the individual in modern society."

There are those, on the other hand, who would deny Servetus any connection with Unitarianism. Jerome Friedman contends that Unitarians are misguided when they claim Servetus as their founder or forerunner. Basing his case on the content of Servetus's theological writings, he argues that Servetus, while a heretic, was in no way a Unitarian. Friedman claims that Unitarian historians have been practicing a sort of pious deceit by covering up Servetus's later work, *The Restitution of Christianity*, and rebuilding Servetus's ideas along proto-Unitarian lines, referring only to his earlier and less systematic *On the Errors of the Trinity*.

Much of the criticism of traditional Unitarian and Unitarian-Universalist historical treatment of Servetus comes from those who cannot relate the doctrines of Servetus to later Unitarian and Universalist ideas. This view seems to be based on the idea that doctrines, such as strict unitarianism, are central to modern Unitarianism and Unitarian Universalism. The liberal religious tradition does not, however, demand any specific set of beliefs. Unitarians and Universalists today hold quite different views on many doctrinal points from their institutional ancestors of just two centuries ago. Yet no one would even think to deny those historical connections.

While critics are no doubt correct when they argue that many liberals have never troubled to understand the whole thought of Servetus, I contend that Servetus belongs to the Unitarian-Universalist tradition on the basis of his story alone. The major theme of this story has been, and continues to be, one of sacrifice.

~

Sacrifice, ritual and historical

Sacrifice is a communal understanding of a death. In this it differs from tragedy, which is the result of an individual's attempt to find fulfillment. Sacrifice always points to a meaning that embodies the values of the community. Thus, a sacrifice lends meaning, not only to the life of the victim, but to the lives of every member of the community.

To begin my analysis, I offer a definition of ritual sacrifice, which I have formed from a study of ancient cultures and from reading the literature on sacrifice in the field of Comparative Religion. Ritual sacrifice is *an intentional killing, performed by publicly designated agents in a sacred context, which is done for a public purpose: to obtain benefits essential for the survival of the community.*

Now the concept of *historical sacrifice*, as opposed to *ritual sacrifice*, allows us to uncover the sacrificial meaning contained in events that may not have been intended as ritual sacrifices. When we look back at an event that has already taken place and decide to treat it as a sacrifice, we have access to the wisdom and emotional power associated with ritual sacrifice, without having to perpetrate a fresh sacrificial killing.

A sacrificial interpretation of an event imbues it with profound meaningfulness. The ability to discern the operation of sacrifice in events that might otherwise seem chaotic, frightening, and meaningless helps to lend shape and dignity to the stories of lives ended tragically and provides a healing power for communities torn by conflict.

The death of Jesus is generally conceded to be a historical event. The Christian interpretation of the event as sacrifice is, in a sense, a model of the kind of theological historical interpretation that I intend to pursue in my analysis of the death of Servetus. The spiritualization, symbolization, and internalization of sacrifice that is represented by the Christian ideal of self-giving serves as an example of how the idea of sacrifice might be integrated into non-ritual thinking and behavior.

There are two communities involved in historical sacrifice. The first is that in which the original event took place. The second is the community in which the story is told. In order to understand an event as historical sacrifice, a new definition is needed, one which takes both communities into account. Just as the later community is in some respect descended from the earlier one, so the definition of historical sacrifice is derived from the definition of communal ritual sacrifice. In order to understand how my original definition may be transformed, let us examine it term by term:

An intentional killing...

The intentional killing took place in the earlier community. It need not have been a sacrifice, in the ritual sense, for this community. The later community has the task of interpreting, understanding, and coming to terms with the event, by using the concepts and meanings associated with sacrifice.

...performed by publicly designated agents...

The task here is to establish how a later community might have a sense of agency in a killing that typically took place many years earlier. This can happen because the earlier community is part of the history and tradition of the later one. It does not matter whether the people in the later society are genetically descended from the earlier one: cultural descent is enough. The earlier community, by virtue of being perceived as part of the story of the later one, is also seen as being contained in it. Therefore, those in the original society who committed the killing with the motive of preserving that society were, by extension, intended benefactors of the society that descended from it.

The participants in the original event—killers and victim—cannot be labeled as good or evil, guilty or innocent. If this were possible, the event could only be described as a crime. A sacrifice is not a crime. Rather, sacrifice provides a mechanism for transcending the categories of guilt and innocence. The later society feels implicated in the killing without being exactly guilty, and it feels a sense of identification with the victim without being entirely innocent.

...in a sacred context...

In a religious ritual, the sense of sacred time and space must be established at the outset. The sacred context is provided for the later community by myth. Myths are sacred stories that have a direct effect on the present. Nevertheless, a story could be given the aura of a myth, even though it was based on a historical incident. And an event need not be distorted to become mythic. The patterns of myth are woven into our activities both public and private all the time. Notable events do not need to be changed in telling to become conformable with myth. They merely need to have the mythic patterns elicited from them. Therefore, if an event is to be called a historical sacrifice, it needs to be perceived by the later community in the form of a mythic story which suggests ritual sacrifice.

...which is for a public purpose: to obtain benefits essential for the survival of the community.

The original event, the killing that took place in the earlier community, may have had a purpose that was related to the preservation of that community, at least in the minds of those who planned, approved and executed the deed. However, in order for the event to stand as a historical sacrifice for the later community, it has to serve a purpose related to the existence of this subsequent society.

The story or myth of the killing must embody values or symbols that are central elements of the ethos and tradition of the later culture. These values define the identity and structure of the later community and express its purpose and meaning. The story could then be said to preserve the later community by providing a vision of its essential character, which allows the community's values to be memorable, communicable, and preservable as well as directly available for both intellectual and emotional response.

Therefore, I define historical sacrifice as *the relationship between an intentional killing, performed in an earlier community in order to ensure its preservation; and a later community, which interprets itself as descended from the earlier community, and which tells the story of the killing in the form of a myth that embodies its essential values.*

Definitions tested

The proposition that the death of Servetus was a sacrifice may then be tested by examining the definitions of ritual and historical sacrifice, again phrase by phrase. I have organized the argument under the following headings:

1. An intentional killing
2. A ritual killing
3. Performance by authorized agents in the earlier community to ensure its preservation
4. Descent of the later community from the earlier community
5. The mythical form of the story
6. The essential values for the later community that are contained in the myth

Ritual sacrifice in the earlier community, Geneva, can be established by the first three of these arguments. Historical sacrifice for the Unitarian Universalist community requires the first, fourth though sixth, and a weaker form of the third—that is to say, the killing agents may have been, but need not have been, authorized.

An Intentional Killing

At eleven o'clock on October 27, 1553, the Lieutenant General and an entourage of officials and guards arrived in Servetus's cell and invited him to accompany them to hear the will of the Council of Geneva. He was brought before the town hall, where he and the Council listened to the Syndic read the charges and the verdict from the balcony. As the recitation ended, a staff was broken over the prisoner. Servetus knelt and begged for a more merciful form of death, but this was denied.

A procession of mounted officials and archers then escorted Servetus, also accompanied by the minister Guillaume Farel, down the rue St. Antoine, through the city gate, to a hill three quarters of a mile south of the city. All along the way, Farel exhorted him to confess his theological errors. A large crowd gathered behind the procession and followed it to the place of execution at Champel.

At the sight of the stake, Servetus fell to the ground to pray, a sight which Farel interpreted as possession by the devil. When he had finished, Servetus rose and took a few steps towards the stake, whereupon he was taken in charge by the executioner and forced to sit on a block while he was chained to the stake and a rope was tied tightly around his neck. His books were tied to the stake with him. He was given a crown of straw and leaves which were sprinkled with sulphur. The executioner held the torch directly in front of his face causing Servetus to cry out. The witnesses murmured in horror. Then the pile of green wood was lit. Servetus moaned and prayed in his unorthodox fashion. Then he fell silent. He remained alive for half an hour in the flames. Finally, the onlookers added enough fuel to the fire so that his body was shortly reduced to ashes.

A Ritual Killing

This account of the death of Servetus highlights some of the highly ritualized features of the arrest, trial and execution. Details from this story can be compared to those from descriptions of ancient animal or human sacrifice ritual.

The ancients found it desirable to have some token of consent or acquiescence to the sacrifice from the victim. There are several points at which Servetus gives a formal consent to his death. First, he came to Geneva when he could have fled to some other place. Further, he came to church where he would be the most conspicuous. When he was given the 'choice' of returning to Vienne he refused. Finally, his steadfast refusal to return to orthodoxy marked him as a self-confessed heretic.

One might argue that Servetus did not really know the risks involved in coming to Geneva, and that he did not really intend to be recognized there at all. The option of returning to Vienne and the inquisition was equivalent to choosing an even more certain death. Returning to orthodoxy would have been an admission of guilt, also punishable by death. All of the tokens of consent might be considered quite differently from Servetus's point of view.

The point of view that counts, however, is that of the society that performs the sacrifice. The ancient Greeks chose to interpret an animal's nod, provoked by a sprinkling of water, as a sign of consent; by the same token, as far as the Reformers of Switzerland were concerned, Servetus was 'asking for it.' He came to Geneva of his own free will, allowed himself to be taken, chose not to be extradited back to France, and provoked his prosecutors and jurors with his wild opinions and obstinacy. This to them was more than enough for a nominal consent.

The responsibility for the accusations was passed from Nicolas de la Fontaine to Antoine Calvin, and finally Calvin himself emerged to help the prosecution. The prosecution itself passed through several hands, including those of Rigot, who was one of the opponents of Calvin in Geneva. The judgment itself passed from the Geneva Council to the Catholics in Vienne and later to the Protestant cities in Switzerland. These passages of responsibility resemble the passing of the axe, and later the blame, in the ancient Greek ox sacrifice. All of society by this means became implicated in the deed.

The breaking of the staff over Servetus resembles the consecrating violence of thrown barley or the cutting of the forelock of an animal victim. Servetus wore a crown of straw. Wreaths or garlands were traditional ceremonial headgear for victims and sacrificers alike.

According to Calvin's ideas, the city of Geneva was a Commonwealth of God, which, to preserve the honor of God, ought to be kept pure of sin. Servetus, polluted by the sin of his heresy, entered Geneva and even profaned a church. Like a ritual scapegoat Servetus was beaten by a blow from a staff, then led ceremoniously in procession outside of the city, beyond the limits of the community. There he was reduced to ashes in the manner of an expiatory or purificatory sacrifice, a burnt offering.

Performed by Authorized Agents in An Earlier Community in Order to Ensure Its Preservation

The death of Michael Servetus was not a criminal act. He was executed by the authority of the Council of Geneva which had unanimously sentenced him to death. The sentence was not pronounced until the other Swiss Reformed churches and councils had been consulted. These communities concurred in the condemnation. The charges that comprised the final verdict were both theological: anti-trinitarianism and anti-paedobaptism. The trial had been largely conducted in the manner of theological debate; therefore Calvin, who had initiated the charges in August, was a consultant to the prosecution. Thus several levels of authority endorsed the burning of Servetus: civil, ecclesiastical, and international.

The burghers of Geneva had a number of reasons for wishing to execute Servetus. Their city was a small and vulnerable state that bordered on the territories of a number of more powerful states that would have liked to incorporate it into their domain. The burghers had managed to free themselves from the overlordship of the Duchy of Savoy only a generation before. They had needed the military aid of Bern to prevent the Savoyard invasion of 1535 from undoing their civil reformation. Subservience to Bern was barely avoided following the end of this menace; it was not until after the death of Servetus that the power of this neighboring Swiss city ceased to loom over Genevan affairs.

The source of many of the reformers that came to Geneva, Bern frequently interfered in the religious affairs of neighboring cities. Under Calvin, Geneva had begun to chart its own course. Its citizens treasured independence, and did not wish to do anything that would threaten their freedom. Even Calvin's opponents did not wish to lose him or to do without the authority and dignity that he brought to Genevan affairs. During a period in which Calvin had been exiled, Bernese influence had increased and religious morale had declined. Thus the burghers understood that they had to defend both the dignity of their own reformation and the effectiveness of their celebrated reformer.

The Catholics were no less a threat. Geneva borders on France. The nearest Swiss city, Fribourg, was Catholic and had also attempted to interfere in Genevan affairs. Cardinal Sadoleto was assigned the task of recapturing the republic for the old faith. To combat these external threats, the city of Geneva acted to prove that it was above reproach, whether by Catholic or Protestant standards. The Reformed Church as a whole, which was tenuously established in a few cities on the borders of major Catholic powers, felt, no less than the city and church of Geneva, the need to prove its orthodoxy and respectability in the face of Catholic criticism. In 1553 the permanency of their reformation could not have seemed at all assured.

The Councillors of Geneva were genuinely shocked by the opinions and behavior of Servetus as reported to them and as they witnessed them during the hearings. Although they did not understand all the details of the theological debate, they did understand that the opinions of Servetus were such as might upset the precarious religious consensus of their state. Their concerns lay in the maintenance of social order, which they believed would be subverted by the ideas of heretics.

Servetus's attack on infant baptism must have seemed particularly threatening to Genevans. If this sacrament were to be rejected, how would the continuity of the church be ensured past the first generation? This was a matter of concern for an embattled community struggling to establish itself. There was also concern for the fate of the soul. The spreading of heresy was considered to be the wholesale slaughter of eternal souls, and thus one of the most heinous crimes imaginable in the 16th century.

Calvin certainly played upon this latter theme in his apologetic. But the main purpose of Calvin's activity in this affair (as in most others) was to preserve the honor of God. He did this largely by maintaining the purity of the church and its doctrines. Calvin placed particular emphasis on the purity of the Holy Supper. In Calvin's eyes, Servetus affronted the honor of God by threatening to instill heretical ideas amongst members of the Geneva church, who if they participated in the sacraments would sully them.

Calvin defended his reformed church in controversy with Catholics by asserting that it was not a novelty or an innovation. He traced the lineage of the true church in such a way as to represent his own, and not the Roman church, as the true inheritors of the ancient traditions. This line of argument would have become harder to maintain if the Genevan church countenanced the presence of a man universally conceded to be a heretic. The French Catholics had already condemned Servetus. Any less zeal for purity than that of the Roman church, which he regarded as itself fallen, would have been unthinkable for Calvin.

Thus Calvin and the Genevans had strong political and religious reasons to burn Servetus. It was an execution, since criminal and theological offenses were both punishable by the civil authorities. It was also a *purification,* as *it* was seen as a cleansing of

Geneva and of Christendom of the miasma created by
blasphemous heretical teachings.

While 16th-century Geneva was perpetually in
danger from the outside, there were periods when
dissention within constituted greater danger. Servetus
arrived at the height of a power struggle between
Calvin and the civil government. The Council, at that
time controlled by a faction called the Libertines,
which was Calvin's particular nemesis, was at that
time attempting to take over the power of
excommunication from the Church Consistory.
Calvin saw this as a direct attack on the purity of the
church, and consequently the honor of God. Just
before the arrival of Servetus, the threat to Calvin's
authority seemed so great that Calvin offered to
resign rather than be a party to the profanation of the
church and its sacraments.

Some of Calvin's enemies may have seen the
arrival of Servetus as a further opportunity to harass
Calvin and to limit his power. Thus Calvin was
involved in two crises at once. He won them both,
however. On September 3, 1553 he prevented one of
his principal opponents, the excommunicate Philip
Berthelier, from taking the sacrament. Then in
October, to protect Geneva from external threats, the
Libertines lined up with their colleagues in
government and joined in the condemnation of
Servetus. In this way the opposition was broken, and
the former opponents forced to participate in the

destruction of Servetus. The death of Servetus, in
effect, had established a new consensus in the city.
The burning was thus, in the context of Geneva in
1553, both an execution and an effective ritual human
sacrifice.

A part of what makes the killing of Servetus seem
so reprehensible to us today is the fact that we are
unconvinced by the reasoning that led the clergy and
the councillors of Geneva and four other cities to pass
their sentence of death. But the perils of their
situation must have seemed quite real to these
Reformed church leaders, charged with preserving
their communities and their faith. They could only
have taken such a drastic step (and which for the
Libertines was against their own factional best
interest) if they believed the welfare and survival of
the community were at stake.

The irony of this preservation of the Geneva
community is that the great contribution of Calvinism
in coming centuries would not be made through the
creation of a uniform godly community. The killing
of Servetus and deaths of countless other Reformation
martyrs would ultimately lead to the privatization of
theology and the separation of church and state. This
is a process that has been brought about by liberal and
orthodox Calvinists alike. The burning of Servetus
represents for the Reformed Church a road only partly
taken, the kind of sacrifice that reminds the people of

God how easy, and disastrous, it would be to revert to the ways of the Middle Ages.

The danger remains for Calvinism, and for any in the United States or any other country, where the call comes forth for the establishment of a Christian state. Historian Heiko Oberman, reflecting on the burning of Servetus by the people of Geneva, wrote:

> Christianity in general, and Calvinism in particular, again become a virulent danger, however, when its adherents, perplexed by the problems of modernity, become nostalgic for the fleshpots of Egypt, that is, for the establishment by force of the visible Kingdom of God. Where Calvinist politics and theology want to be more than a witness mediated by an individual's own life and sacrificial spirit, there they have crossed the fatal boundary line between influence and coercive power, and we can smell again the first wisps of the smoke rising from the stake.

A Later Community, Which Interprets Itself As Descended from The Earlier Community

Here I mean specifically the Liberal church represented by Unitarians and Unitarian Universalists, though as I have already indicated the benefits of Servetus's sacrifice need not be thought limited to us, but may be extended to Calvinists generally. I will not expand on our descent from Calvin and the Reformed

Church of Geneva, for I do not wish to recover the too much of same material that Andrew Hill has already presented for us.

To add an American point of view, however, let me briefly quote historian Conrad Wright on the subject. He thought that though Unitarians differed from more orthodox Calvinists,

> ...the frame of reference within which all these issues [God, human nature, the Trinity] were disputed was the reformed theology of the Westminster Confession. The liberals gave unorthodox answers, but the questions were not unorthodox questions. If the liberals were unorthodox in their responses, they were nevertheless quite orthodox in accepting those questions as the important ones that had to be addressed. This means that one of the most important factors in the shaping of Unitarianism was the theology of John Calvin. As between Calvin and Servetus, or Calvin and the Socini, who has the greatest influence on American Unitarianism? Which one is the ancestor? Calvin, of course.

Which Tells The Story of The Killing in The Form of A Myth

Many of the myths of Unitarian Universalism are to be found in the accounts of certain historical events. One of these is the story of Servetus. I know it

is mythic because I have heard a set of stories of
Servetus which are only partially coordinated with the
known facts. These stories tell more about Unitarian
Universalism than they do about Servetus. Their
principal goal is to interpret and guide the religious
and social life of those who belong to the community
of the myth; critically accurate history is a secondary
goal. The telling of these stories brings an immediacy
to its listeners. The shock, the horror, the outrage, and
the guilt are all very vivid. The myth defines an
audience: those who react in a certain set of ways to
the story, who are motivated by it to elevate certain
ideals. It is a sacred story, told reverently at the
beginning of any general Unitarian Universalist
historical account. Once this foundational sacrificial
myth is told, the connected history of Unitarianism
can begin.

A Myth That Embodies Its Essential Values

Earl Morse Wilbur identifies the three controlling
principles of the Unitarian movement as freedom,
tolerance, and reason. In the story of Servetus,
although all three are present, the value that the story
of Servetus has come to embody for Western culture
at large is tolerance. While religious intolerance did
not cease after 1553 (nor did it diminish for a
century), the questions that Sebastian Castellio and
others began to ask shortly after the execution of
Servetus were the beginning of our modern attitudes
on theological and religious diversity. The Geneva

event came to stand for all of the many killings due to religious persecution.

Tolerance allows freedom of conscience to flourish. Servetus did not allow his conscience to be compromised or violated by the forces of coercion. Theophilus Lindsey, one of the founders of British Unitarian movement in the 18th century, wrote, "Surely it was much to his honour, that neither intreaties *[sic]*, nor the near prospect of the most horrible sufferings could induce him to say or do any thing against his conscience."

The history of Unitarian Universalism starts from this tragic episode and works towards progressively more tolerant ways of dealing with religious disagreement. The story of Theodore Parker's troubles with other Unitarian ministers in Boston in the 1840s represents another stage along the road towards constructive accommodation. We have not, of course, arrived at a perfect state of pluralistic accord. If we had, the story of Servetus and Calvin as myth would have lost much of its power and necessity, and might cease to be told. The Servetus story does not merely point out our accomplishment as liberals, but indicates a direction in which we must continue to move. Our charge is to seek to overcome the disharmony in our diversity by working through it rather than by eliminating it.

Now, in order to demonstrate the sacrificial role of Servetus in our history it was not necessary to analyze his theology. Therefore, we can continue to claim Servetus as part of our tradition regardless of what we discover about his beliefs. There is no need for us to continue to force 'unitarian' readings of his treatises, if that would distort his intended meaning. We can now dare to become truly acquainted with the ideas and message of this man, whose story means so much to us in terms of our values and tradition. Disencumbered of prejudice as to what we should find out about his antitrinitarianism, I think we will continue to discover new evidence that he was, in other ways, as in his rejection of original sin and vicarious atonement, a stimulating precursor of modern liberal thought.

The fact that we can claim Servetus as a central figure in our tradition without reference to his theology further demonstrates one of our most basic principles: the commitment to freedom of belief and the rejection of any creedal test for inclusion in our denomination. We are reminded that there is no theological way to determine from the outside whether any person, past or present, really belongs within or without our denomination. In this way, as well as in our rejection of Calvin's method of purifying the community by destroying heretics, the story helps us to define our identity.

The sacrifice of Servetus reminds us of the seriousness of our religious quest. If our own faith tradition is built on sacrifice, we must strive to be worthy inheritors of that which was born in ashes and blood. We must also remember that each person who joins a Unitarian or Unitarian-Universalist church is choosing to take on not only the benefits that Servetus's sacrifice provides but a share of the responsibility for what happened to him.

~

Heroic Consequences

The story of Servetus, as often told in the Unitarian and Universalist tradition, reveals a deep antipathy to Calvin. This may indicate a desire on the part of many Unitarians and Unitarian Universalists to entirely distinguish their denominations from the Calvinist one from which they emerged. Some individuals may also wish to use the story to symbolically separate themselves from their more orthodox Christian upbringing. The depth of feeling involved in the rejection of another faith may be felt in the isolation, persecution, and final agony of the heretic Servetus.

The danger of such thinking is that the Calvinist church may be improperly *externalized* and demonized. The Calvin–Servetus story represents an *internal* struggle between the powers of puritanism and radicalism, within our own Protestant-born tradition and within our own souls. We distort the meaning of the story if we use it to justify rejecting a portion of the tradition that is in fact our own. An understanding of the sacrificial nature of the execution of Servetus can help us to accept the event in its totality. This interpretation enables us to own our inheritance from Calvin by allowing us to see his actions as a necessary part of the sacrifice that preserved and defines our cherished modern community. It frees us from the need to reject the misguided Calvin and the embattled Geneva community as villains or to idealize the provocative Servetus as the only hero.

Servetus, in fact, makes a very ambiguous hero. On the one hand, he was inquisitive, intelligent, talented, and high-principled. At the same time, he was stubborn, eccentric, and erratic, often hysterical, and always disputatious. He demanded to be heard, but was capable of shouting an opponent down. And these flaws in the character of Servetus are an important feature of his story. He was not *by character* a hero, but he *attained* heroism in the end. He may have exhibited flaws of character in the conduct of his life, but he is remembered for the integrity and the dignity of his death.

The sacrificial aspect of the story reminds us of the capacity for deeds of great nobility that abides in every person, however flawed and fallible. It teaches us that it is never too late to find fulfillment, to make a difference in the world, and to become an inspiration to later generations. It offers us the hope that, in the face of a crisis, we too may discover within ourselves unknown resources of courage, and that we too may witness for truth, even at the expense of our own lives.

~

SOURCES

ALLEN, Joseph Henry. *A History of the Unitarians and the Universalists in the United States.* New York: Christian Literature Co., 1894. p.48.
    "The error which looked to [his prosecutors] so flagrant they hoped to burn away in his funeral pile. But his truth is saved for us by that very fire, which tries every man's work of what sort it is. For, without that baleful light, it would doubtless have perished with him."

BAINTON, Roland. *Hunted Heretic.* Boston: Beacon Press, 1953. pp.170–81.

CALVIN, John. "Articles concerning the Organization of the Church and of Worship at Geneva proposed by the Ministers at the Council, January 16, 1537," in *Calvin, Theological Treatises,* trans. J. K. S. Reid, in The Library of Christian Classics. Philadelphia: Westminster, 1954. p.50.
———. *Institutes of the Christian Religion,* 1559. Book 4.

CASTELLIO, Sebastian. *Concerning Heretics,* trans. Roland Bainton. New York: Columbia University Press, 1935. pp.266–67, 277.

"What preposterous humanity is it, I ask you, to cover with silence the crime of one man and to prostitute a thousand souls to the snares of Satan?" (CALVIN, quoted in, p.266.)

"What will become of religion? By what marks will the true Church be discerned? What will Christ himself be if the doctrine of piety is uncertain and in suspense?" (Excerpt from CALVIN's *Defensio orthodoxae fidei,* quoted by Sebastian Castellio in his *Contra libellum Calvini.* p.267.)

"Shall the whole body of Christ be mangled that one putrid member remain intact?" (CALVIN, quoted in, p.277)

FRIEDMAN, Jerome. *Michael Servetus: A Case Study in Total Heresy*. Geneva: Librairie Droz, 1978. pp.14–15.

FRITCHMAN, Stephen Hole. *Men of Liberty.* Boston: Beacon Press, 1944. p.3.

Fritchman portrays the burning of Servetus in Calvin's Geneva as the, "flames seen round the world...The burning of Servetus at the stake," he wrote, "can be said to have started the Unitarian movement."

FROTHINGHAM, Octavius Brooks. *Theodore*

Parker, A Biography, 1874. p.206.

FULTON, John F. *Michael Servetus: Humanist and Martyr*. New York: Herbert Reichner, 1953. pp.19, 45.

HILLAR, Marian. *Michael Servetus: Intellectual Giant, Humanist, and Martyr*. Lanham, Maryland: University Press of America, 2002. p.xxii.

HOPFT, Harro. *The Christian Polity of John Calvin*. Cambridge: Cambridge University Press, 1982. pp.129–38.

HUGHES, Philip E., ed. *The Register of the Company of Pastors of Geneva in the Time of Calvin*. Grand Rapids: Eerdmans, 1966. p.284.
"Whoever therefore sincerely and prudently considers these things will acknowledge that his object was, by extinguishing the light of sound doctrine, to overthrow the whole of religion."

LINDSEY, Theophilus. *An Historical View of the State of the Unitarian Doctrine and Worship*. London: J. Johnson, 1783. pp.282–83.

OBERMAN, Heiko A. *The Two Reformations*. New Haven: Yale University Press, 2003. p.156.

PARKER, T. H. L. *John Calvin: A Biography*. Philadelphia: Westminster, 1975. pp.54–126.

PARKER, Theodore. "The Nebraska Question: some thoughts upon the new assault upon freedom in America," in *Collected Works of Theodore Parker,* vol.5. London: Trubner, 1865. p.247.
————. "Sermons of theism, atheism, and the popular theology," in *Collected Works of Theodore Parker,* vol.11. London: Trubner, 1865. pp.xxxvii, 3, 76, 86, 243.

WEISS, John. *Life and Correspondence of Theodore Parker,* vol. 1. New York: Appleton, 1864. p.360.

WILBUR, Earl Morse. *A History of Unitarianism,* 2 vols. Boston: Beacon Press.
————. vol.1: *Socinianism and Its Antecedents,* 1945. p.210.
    Wilbur spoke of, "the impulse that his tragic death gave to the growth of toleration in religion."
————. vol.2: *In Transylvania, England, and America,* 1952. p.486.

WILLIS, Robert. *Servetus and Calvin: A Study of an Important Epoch in the Early History of the Reformation.* London: Henry S. King, 1877. pp.x, 488.

WRIGHT, Conrad, ed. *A Stream of Light.* Boston: Unitarian Universalist Association, 1975. p.xii.
    It is noteworthy that this statement is found in what is still the most current, official history of the American Unitarian movement.

WRIGHT, Richard. *Apology for Dr. Michael
Servetus*. Wisbech, Cambridgeshire: F. B. Wright,
1806. pp.353–55.

A Martyr Soul Remembered:
Commemorating the 450th Anniversary of the
Death of Michael Servetus

DAY III

Sunday, 26th October 2003

— ~ —

MORNING: Chapelle des Crêts

AFTERNOON: The Old City

EVENING: Centre International Reformé
John Knox

5

SERVETUS, SCIENCE, AND THE BREATH OF GOD: HONOURING SERVETUS IN 2003*

Richard Boeke
Minister, Horsham, West Sussex, and
President of the World Congress of Faiths

— ~ —

A war of civilizations! That is how many see the beginning of the 21st century since the birth of Jesus, 'the Prince of Peace'. As we enter the struggle of faiths that is the 21st century, it is fitting to remember another who gave his life for what he saw to be the truth of his science and his religion: Michael Servetus, burned at the stake as a heretic 450 years ago.

"Jesus, thou son of the eternal God, have pity on me," were the last words of Michael Servetus as he was burned at the stake in Geneva, Switzerland, on

*__*Preached at the Chapelle des Crêts, Chemin des Crêets de Pregny, Geneva, on Sunday, 26th October 2003.__*

the 27th October 1553. John Calvin approved the execution with the recommendation that Servetus be beheaded, not burned alive. But like Joan of Arc and Jan Hus, it was the flames for heretics. As Servetus said, "Jesus, thou son of the eternal God...," it is recorded that Farel, one of Calvin's fellow ministers, said in effect, "If he would only say 'eternal Son of God,' we could cut him free." If he would only affirm that God was three separate persons, he would no longer be a Christian heretic.

Michael Servetus was born in Spain in 1511. He studied law and religion at Toulouse, and medicine in Paris. In his study of the human body, he discovered the pulmonary circulation of the blood: that the blood goes through the lungs, is renewed by air, and returns to the heart to be pumped out through the arteries. He discovered the link between air and life.

In most religions, 'breath' is a metaphor for God, "Breathe on me Breath of God, fill me with life anew." In Hinduism, Prajapati, the primal spirit, is asked how many gods there are. He tells of over 19,000 names recorded. Then he says, "In truth, there is only one God, 'Breath.'" Without breath, no other Gods exist.

When the American civil rights leader, Martin Luther King, Jr., was a student at Boston University, the dean of the University Chapel was Howard Thurman, a grandson of slaves. Years later, after

King had been knifed in New York City, he asked to see Thurman. When Thurman arrived at the hospital, King was reading Thurman's book, *Jesus and the Dispossessed.*

Since Thurman was a black man, he was often mistaken for the janitor despite his office as Boston University's Dean of the Chapel. A rabbi tells the story of driving early each day to the university and standing in the hall of the chapel to say his Hebrew prayers before classes. A man he took to be the janitor invited him into the chapel. The rabbi pointed to the cross and explained he could not pray there. The next morning when the rabbi arrived, the cross was gone, but the rabbi still would not enter. The 'janitor' invited him in once more. As the rabbi refused again, the 'janitor' replied, "Don't you believe in the Ruach Hagofen, the Breath of the Holy?" The rabbi discovered that the 'janitor' was none other than Howard Thurman, the dean of the Chapel. Each day after that, the rabbi prayed in the chapel.

Thurman was the living link between Mahatma Gandhi and Martin Luther King, Jr. In the mid-1930s, Thurman and his wife toured India on behalf of the YMCA. Gandhi invited Thurman to come for a day. They talked for hours, Gandhi trying to understand how Thurman could accept Christianity, given the way white Christians often treated African

Americans. Near the end of the visit, Gandhi asked
the Thurmans to sing a favourite hymn,

> Were you there when they crucified my Lord?
> Sometimes, it causes me to tremble, tremble,
>   tremble,
> Were you there when they crucified my Lord?

Gandhi and Thurman shared the Ruach Hagofen,
the Breath of the Holy, the universal which inspires
all particular religions. The Holy is recorded in many
forms and many scriptures.

Near our Unitarian Chapel in Horsham is the
Shelley Fountain. Like Servetus, Shelley rejected the
church of his time and looked for universals in nature.
The Shelley Fountain reflects the spirit of Shelley's
poem, 'The Cloud':

> I am the daughter of Earth and Water,
>   and the nursling of the Sky.
> I pass through the pores of the ocean
>   and shores,
> I change, but cannot die.

Shelley's poem helps me to imagine the different
appearances of the divine. Water can be a river, or it
can be snow or ice. It can be invisible in the air, or it
can be a dark cloud as we sing, "Raindrops keep
falling on my head...."! The Greek God, Zeus, dwelt
in the clouds of Mt. Olympus. The Hebrew image of

God was inspired by clouds, "His chariots of wrath the deep thunderclouds form, and dark is his path on the wings of the storm." Or the more gentle words, "God is a spirit, and they that worship… worship in spirit and in truth." As the Bible begins, we are told, "God breathed into the human form, and the human form became a living soul."

For Servetus, through the lungs, the breath of God is breathed into us. Our blood carries the divine spirit to every part of our body. So, Hebrew scripture forbids the eating of blood, for blood contains the soul of the animal. The early Church transformed the seder shared by Jesus and his disciples. It became the Catholic Mass by which we share the soul of Jesus by eating his flesh and drinking his blood.

Servetus affirmed the sacrament of communion, but with the spiritual not the physical presence of Christ. There was no physical change in the elements brought about by transubstantiation. The other sacrament that Servetus affirmed was baptism, but only for adults as a sign of spiritual regeneration. His rejection of infant baptism makes him a spiritual ancestor of Baptists and Unitarians. It was the second heresy for which he was burned at the stake.

His first heresy was the denial of the Trinity. At the age of 20, Servetus had published his book, *On the Errors of the Trinity*. It was printed in Alsace, near what later would be the boyhood home of another heretic named Albert Schweitzer. Like Schweitzer, Servetus wished to get to the historical Jesus, not the abstract Trinity of the Church. The Holy Spirit is not a separate being, but an action of God animating all life. As Jesus was filled with the Holy Spirit, he became the Son of God. While God is eternal, Jesus is not eternal, but became the Son of God in his lifetime.

The new invention of the printing press was providing texts, which opened minds. Servetus had studied a newly printed edition of the New Testament in Greek. And reading the original Greek, Servetus realized that the doctrine of God as three separate people is not in the Bible. The early Greek church fathers wrote of God as having three 'masks' like an actor in a Greek drama. In Greek, the masks of the actors are called 'persona.' Translated into Latin this became three 'individuals.' For Servetus, the power of the One God animates all things. Even the devil is of God. In today's terms Servetus could be seen as a kindred spirit to Matthew Fox and Creation Theology. Not that Nature is God. Rather God is in nature, animating all things.

God has many names. Which would you lose: heart, lung or brain? Remember in *The Wizard of Oz,* the Scarecrow, the Cowardly Lion, the Tin Man, each missing a vital part? God is the Divine energy of the whole.

Servetus, like da Vinci, was a Renaissance man. Four hundred and fifty years ago the high specialization in science and the scientific method did not exist. It was common that the theologian, the scientist, the alchemist and the philosopher were the same person. He lived in the time of Galileo and Copernicus. Like them, he was attacked by Church authorities for scientific studies that conflicted with the teaching of the Church. Like Newton, 100 years later, Servetus saw himself as an interpreter of Divine History, linking the insights of scripture to the revelations of God in nature.

Keys to understanding Servetus

In his book, *Hunted Heretic,* Professor Roland Bainton of Yale reminds us that the scientific findings of Servetus are announced in a work of theology. For Servetus, theology, science and art were not compartmentalized. This Classical and Renaissance approach to reality as a whole is the first key to understanding Servetus. In examining nature, we are exploring the riddle of the universe. In examining scripture, we seek the original meaning of what was written.

The second key to understanding Servetus is his rejection of the mechanical, impersonal universe of the Stoics. His belief was close to the 'élan vital', the vital force of French philosopher Henri Bergson. Like Bergson's *Creative Evolution,* Servetus saw the universe as filled with dynamic and creative energy.

The universe is filled with the Holy Spirit, the very essence of God. Servetus looked for clues to the heavens like Kepler and Gallieo, and to the human body like Vesalius and Harvey. When Emerson says, "The task of the preacher is not to say that God spoke, but rather that God speaketh," Servetus could say, "Amen."

The third key to understanding Servetus is his passion to be part of the Kingdom of God. Here is 'the impossible dream' that carries Jesus to the cross and Schweitzer to Africa. For those possessed by 'the impossible dream', it is not enough to comprehend God by reason, or to accept the grace of God by faith.

For Servetus, as for George Fox and the Quakers, we are possessed of an 'inner light'. Servetus declared, "Our soul is a certain light of God, a spark of the spirit of God, an innate light of divinity."

The soul is breathed into the human form by God. As the air purifies the blood, so God inspires the soul. As Servetus discovered the role of the lungs in renewing the blood, he grasped the teaching of the Torah that the soul is in the blood. It is not static in the heart or brain. It moves through the whole person. Servetus writes, "By the breath of God…within the heart and soul of Adam and his children, the Spirit, the spark of the Holy, was joined with the blood and the soul was made."

Here is faith in the unity of all Reality. Everything is connected. With the poet Tennyson, Servetus could have said,

> Flower in the crannied wall,
> I pluck you out of the crannies…
> … if I could understand
> What you are, root and all…
> I should know what God and man is.

What of these three keys to understanding Servetus?

1. The unity of knowledge;
2. God as dynamic energy;
3. *The Restoration of Christianity*, not Calvin's *Institutes of the Christian Religion.*

These three keys can still inspire those of us who wish to take up the quest and live 'the impossible dream'. To live now as though we are already living in the Commonwealth of God.

Our time is much like that of Servetus, as oil-hungry capitalists use Christian Zionists and radical Muslims to create a climate of fear and terror. They encourage the pseudoscience of Creationism and books like *The Bible Code,* which claim to discover a code in the Torah predicting the events of the 21st century. Servetus would say, "Baloney."

Another resident of Geneva, the philosopher Voltaire, reminds us, "Those who believe absurdities can commit atrocities." We can condemn Calvin for burning Servetus, yet today for the sake of Western civilisation, we slaughter tens of thousands and starve millions. "Eternal God have mercy upon us. Amen."

~

SOURCES

BAINTON, Roland H. "Church history," lectures. New Haven, Yale University, 1952.
————. *Hunted Heretic: The Life and Death of Michael Servetus, 1511-1553.* Boston: Beacon Press, 1953. *See* Bainton's wonderful sketches of the Trinity in this title.

BERGSON, Henri. *Creative Evolution,* English translation. New York, 1911. Memories of Bergson's élan vital were evoked especially because the speaker had been a guest in a home near Geneva that for 30 years was Bergson's summer residence.

BIBLE, King James Version. Genesis 2:7, John 4:24.

DARION, Joe. "To dream the impossible dream," song of Don Quixote in the Leigh–Darion musical, *Man of LaMancha* (book by Dale Wasserman, 1966).

DROSNIN, Michael. *The Bible Code.* New York: Simon & Schuster, 1997.

EMERSON, Ralph Waldo. "Divinity school address," 1838.

GRANT, Robert. "O worship the king," [English hymn, verse 2, as inspired by an Old Testament psalmist,] 1833.

SCHACHTER, Zalman. *The First Step: A Guide for the New Jewish Spirit.* New York: Bantam Books, 1983.

SHELLEY, Percy. "The cloud," in *Prometheus Unbound,* 1820.

TENNYSON, Alfred, Lord. "Flowers in a crannied wall," 1868.

THURMAN, Howard. *Jesus and the Disinherited.* Boston: Beacon Press, 1976.
————. *With Head and Heart: The Autobiography of Howard Thurman.* New York: Harcourt Brace Jovanovich, 1979.

VOLTAIRE, 1767. Cited in, "Casualties of war—first truth, then conscience," by Norman SOLOMON, *Minneapolis–St. Paul Free Press,* 2003 March 20, with the date of the quote and its corrected English wording. Dr. R.B. Meyer believes this

quote should be accepted as a summation of
Voltaire's philosophy rather than a direct one (*see*
http://www.ronaldbrucemeyer.com/rants).

6

SERVETUS IN GENEVA: PLACES TO VISIT*

Clifford M. Reed

— ~ —

1. Site of La Rose d'Or: It was at this inn, on the corner of Place du Molard and rue du Rhône, in the shadow of the Tour du Molard, that Servetus lodged on his arrival in Geneva on 12th or 13th August 1553, after four months on the run from the French Inquisition. As he had asked the innkeeper to arrange transport up the lake, apparently en route to Zurich, it doesn't seem that Servetus intended to stay in Geneva for any length of time. The site of La Rose d'Or is now occupied by 'Zara', a fashionable clothes shop.

2. Temple de la Madeleine: Servetus attended service at this church, where Guillaume Farel was minister, on the afternoon of Sunday, 13th August. Not to have gone to church in Calvin's Geneva would

---

* Sites 1–6 formed the basis for a tour of Old Town on Sunday afternoon. Conference attendees gathered at Sites 7–8 on Monday morning. Refer to the map on page 118.

have aroused suspicion. However, Servetus was recognized—by people who had known him in France—and he was arrested and taken off to prison. The church has undergone major reconstruction since the 16th century.

3. Site of the Bishop's Palace: Following the Reformation, the Bishop's Palace was turned into a prison and courthouse. Servetus was both imprisoned and tried here. He was kept in appalling conditions and only brought from his cell for the show trial that ended with his conviction and condemnation as a heretic on 26th October. The building stood on the rue de l'Évêché in the shadow of the Cathedral. It was later demolished and a prison was built on the site. It is now an open space. Some underground remains of the later prison can be seen, and a display board records that Servetus was incarcerated on the site.

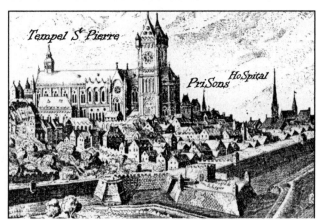

THE WALLS OF GENEVA, 1602.

4. Cathédrale St-Pierre: At the heart of the old town, the cathedral was John Calvin's pulpit from 1536 and became the headquarters of the Calvinist Reformation. Among Calvin's sermon topics in the autumn of 1553 was the denunciation of Michael Servetus, who lay in prison only a short distance away.

5. Hôtel de Ville: Standing on a street to which it gives its name, the historic administrative headquarters of Geneva dates, in parts, from the 15th century. It was here, at 10:00 in the morning of 27th October 1553, that Servetus was brought for final condemnation. The procession to the place of execution in Champel then set out.

6. Monument de la Réformation: Today, a walk from the Hôtel de Ville to Champel could well take in this impressive monument in the Promenade des Bastions, below the rue de la Croix Rouge. Set against the massive 16th-century city walls, the monument was constructed in 1909 to commemorate the 400th anniversary of Calvin's birth.

East of the Place Neuve, the statues in the Promenade des Bastions and inscriptions celebrate the founders and major figures of Reformed Protestant Christianity in Europe and North America including Oliver Cromwell, Roger Williams and the 'Mayflower' pilgrims. Central though are—quite

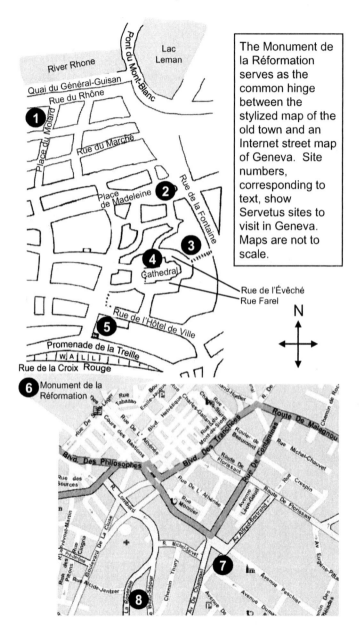

The Monument de la Réformation serves as the common hinge between the stylized map of the old town and an Internet street map of Geneva. Site numbers, corresponding to text, show Servetus sites to visit in Geneva. Maps are not to scale.

literally!—the four 'giants' of Calvinism: John Calvin, Guillaume Farel, Theodore Beza and John Knox. Needless to say, there is no mention of Servetus!

7. Champel: It was to Champel, now a district to the south of the city centre, that Servetus was brought for execution—timed for 12:00 noon—on the 27th October 1553. The ICUU's 450th anniversary service of commemoration began at the Plateau de Champel, a small triangular park at the summit of the rue Michel-Servet, and concluded at his monument down the hill.

8. The Servetus Monument: The monument commemorating Michael Servetus is a simple stone erected in 1903. It stands in a rather obscure spot southwest of where the rue Michel-Servet meets the intersection of av. de le Rosarie and av. de Beau-Séjour. Bearing in mind his rarely acknowledged contribution to medical science, it is appropriate—if not ironic—that the site faces the Cantonal Hospital. This hospital occupies the probable site of Servetus's execution.

~

(left to right) Rev. Marie-Laure Jakubec, Mme. Marianne Wanstall, Rt. Rev. Joel Stroudinsky, Rev. Clifford Reed.

THE SERVETUS MONUMENT, GENEVA

Andrew M. Hill

— ~ —

All previous Servetus monuments—in France and in Spain—had been erected by Catholics, anxious to draw attention to Protestant intolerance. With the 350th anniversary of Servetus's death approaching, there had been talk, especially by Free Thinkers, of erecting a monument in Geneva itself. Aware that this would focus even more attention upon the cruelest episode in the Genevan Reformation, local Protestants were anxious to erect a memorial of their own and—hopefully—thereby deflect more criticism.

But what should the monument's inscription say? What could it say which didn't cast Jean Calvin in too unfavourable a light—and, at the same time, didn't magnify Servetus's alleged errors? In the end, the Calvinist party, led by Emile Domergue, won the day over the pro-Servetus group. The result would be an expiatory monument for a cruel death rather than one that commemorated a martyr. In particular, Unitarians would be kept at bay, although according to Alexander Gordon (1841–1931, principal of the Unitarian Home Missionary College [later, Unitarian College], Manchester, England, 1890–1911), considerable British and American funding was provided behind the scenes.

The monument itself is a rough-hewn granite block. It is in the Champel area outside the old city, and stands on a steep bank in the angle where avenue Beau-Séjour meets avenue de la Rosarie. It overlooks the former Champs du Bourreau (Executioner's Enclosure) where the execution occurred and where the Cantonal Hospital now stands. Close by is rue Michel Servet.

~

On the front, but less accessible side facing avenue de la Rosarie and the hospital, the inscription reads:

LE XXVII OCTOBRE MDLIII
MOVRUT SVR LE BVCHER
A CHAMPEL
MICHEL SERVET
DE VILLENEVVE D'ARAGON
NE LE XXIX SEPTEMBRE MDXI

[The 27th October 1553, died on the pyre at Champel, Michael Servetus de Villeneuve of Aragon, born 29th September 1511.]

On the other, facing avenue Beau-Séjour, the inscription reads:

FILS
RESPECTEUX ET RECONNAISSANTS
DE CALVIN
NOTRE GRAND RÉFORMATEUR
MAIS CONDAMNANT UNE ERREUR
QUI FUT CELLE DE SON SIÈCLE
ET FERMEMENT ATTACHÉS
Á LA LIBERTÉ DE CONSCIENCE
SELON LES VRAIS PRINCIPES
DE LA RÉFORMATION ET DE L'ÉVANGILE
NOUS AVONS ÉLEVÉ
CE MONUMENT EXPIATOIRE
LE XXVII OCTOBRE MCMIII

[Respectful and grateful sons of Calvin our great Reformer, but condemning an error which was made in his time, and being firmly committed to liberty of conscience according to true principles of the Reformation and of the Gospel, we have raised this expiatory monument. The 27th October 1903.]

Each year, on the anniversary of Servetus's death, an unknown person places flowers at the memorial. On 27th October 2003, additional tributes were placed there by a Buddhist, by the City of Geneva, and by the International Council of Unitarians and Universalists.

~

SOURCES

BOEKE, Richard. Photograph, 2003 October. Memorial service participants, from the avenue de la Beau-Séjour.

BRADFORD, Beatrice. *The Little Book of Geneva.* Geneva, Swit.: Librairie Kundig, 1926.

HURLBURT, Esther. Photograph, 2003 October. Memorial stone, rear view from avenue Beau-Séjour.
————. Photograph, 2003 October. Rue Michel-Servet street sign.

REED, Paulette. Photograph, 2003. Memorial stone, front view from avenue de la Rosarie.

Seeing Geneva [running title of an unidentified guide book], pp.94–95, sent to A.M. Hill as photocopies by the late David Brown of Edinburgh and Geneva, ca. 1990.

WILBUR, Earl Morse. *History of Unitarianism [vol.1] Socinianism and its antecedents,* 1945. p.180 n.91, "The precise place of execution was on the west side of the present chemin de Beau-Séjour, where the new clinic now stands, and on the terrace in front of the house and overlooking the chemin de la Roseraie. The expiatory monument erected in 1903 was placed as near this spot as possible, near the bottom of the rue Michel Servet. *Cf.,* E. Domergue, "L'emplacement du Bûcher de Michel Servet." *Bulletin de la Société d'Archéologie de Genève,* 1908 May 2; pp.856–63.

www.multimap.com, 2004 July 19.

ZUBER, Valentine. "Pour en finir avec Michel Servet. Les protestants du début du XXe siècle entre m´moire et histoire (1903)." *Bulletin Société Histoire du Protestanisme Français:* 1995 janvier–février–mars; pp.97–112.

7

THE DRAMA OF SERVETUS

Clifford M. Reed

— ~ —

Imagine the scene. A solemn procession of priests, monks and hooded Inquisitors is arriving at a town square. In the square a stake is set up, surrounded by brushwood, logs and bales of paper. The procession fans out to fill the square, and a figure is dragged forward and bound to the stake. As prayers are said, the pyre is lit and the figure is enveloped in flames. But it is soon clear that the figure, now being reduced to ashes, is not a man but an effigy. Around its neck, creasing and blackening in the flames, is a placard. On it is written one word: 'Servetus.' A caption on the screen reads, 'Vienne, France, December 23rd 1553.'

Such might be the opening of a film, a movie, about Michael Servetus. And I have always thought that his was a life that deserves to have a film made about it. His story is full of drama. It is a true tragedy in that his nature and his personality, when combined with his radical, nonconformist ideas, doomed him from his youth to the fate which awaited him.

Sixteenth-century Europe had no room for a man who challenged the embattled rival orthodoxies that struggled for control of the continent's souls and territories. There is a terrible inevitability to his tale.

The film would then go back nearly thirty years to show us the eager, questioning Spanish youth, and then tell the story from there. His growing discontent with the Church's doctrine. His witnessing the pomp of Pope Clement VII's arrival in Bologna, and his fury and disillusion at what he saw as its idolatry and its betrayal of Christ's simplicity. His flight to the Protestant cities of Switzerland and Germany; the publication of *De Trinitatis Erroribus;* the fury it aroused among Catholic and Protestant alike. The dramatic potential of an angry young man cocking a snook at just about everyone in authority, until forced into hiding, is considerable—but there is a lot more to come!

There are his adventures in Paris, particularly his medical and anatomical studies and the great discovery they led to. The quiet years spent as a physician and editor. The one chance—in Vienne— for bringing a romantic, even sexual, interest into the story; this is a movie after all! But all the time the bubbling up of his desire to 'restore Christianity'; the suspicions surrounding him amongst Catholic and Protestant; the extraordinary circumstances in which *Christianismi Restitutio* is printed. And then things gather pace. His betrayal and arrest. His dramatic escape and flight. Arrest in Geneva. The courtroom drama and the confrontation with Calvin. And then the terrible dénouement at Champel in October 1553, to complete the circle begun in the opening sequence.

Servetus's own complex character; the tensions between his desire to tell the truth as he saw it, and the temptation to opt for the quiet life and safety; the fact that he was no 'plaster saint' and had plenty of faults and failings; his ultimately irrepressible honesty and courage: all these make his an intriguing personality, as are the personalities of those with whom he clashed—notably the towering figure of John Calvin himself.

I don't know whether that film will ever be made! Probably not, I'm sorry to say. But his story—and the issues it raises—has inspired several writers to use it in the context of drama. I certainly make no claim to have a comprehensive knowledge of what drama has been written about Servetus! I know there is a play in French and there have been Spanish contributions to the genre, but I can't tell you much more than that. But I want to say a word about three works that I do have, in whole or in part. We will then hear some extracts from them [these are reproduced in full as appendices, pp.136–175].

"Servetus: A Drama," by Henry Warburton Hawkes [two readers]

Henry Warburton Hawkes (1843–1917) was a British Unitarian minister. He wrote this 'drama' in May 1904, although it was not published in printed form until May 1911. As to where, when or, indeed, whether it was produced on stage, I have no idea. Indeed, I didn't know of its existence until Andrew Hill sent it to me in the run-up to this conference. It is rather an interesting piece of work! It is written in a poetic—even quasi-Shakespearean!—style that may sound rather odd today. It opens with a prologue scene set in Vienne in April 1553. Two of Servetus's friends, Sorel and Farrel, are reminiscing about Servetus, who has been arrested by the Inquisition. A third friend, Clement, enters and tells them that, with his help and that of his girlfriend, Marie (the jailer's daughter), Servetus has escaped.

To general amazement and consternation, Servetus himself then appears, and says he plans to go to Naples—maybe via Geneva. His friends counsel him against this, recalling his own account of Calvin's threats against him, "...if I dared to take my heresies within Geneva's walls...I ne'er should leave alive if he held sway!" Servetus then leaves, with the sounds of hot pursuit already audible.

In **Scene One** proper, set in Geneva, a conversation between Calvin and Beza gives an insight into Calvin's life and character, and into the course of the

Reformation. Later, an acrimonious debate with two of Geneva's Syndics (political leaders), Perrin and Berthelier, gives an idea of the tense and complex political situation into which Servetus walked in Geneva.

Scene Two is set in Servetus's prison cell in Geneva. It begins with a brief soliloquy by Servetus. This begins, "And this is now the end of all my dreams! What madness in my blood has served me so!…What tempter brought me here amongst the foes who hate my very name! …." And concludes,

> It was a futile wish that I might meet
> This old antagonist in free debate
> That lured me to my doom! A madman's
> dream
> The wakening from which awaits me now.

The 'old antagonist' is Calvin, who then enters the cell. Our *first extract* is the conversation that follows. Calvin speaks first. ["Servetus, know'st thou me?" to the end of Scene Two.]

Scene Three is also set in the prison cell, but sometime later, on the eve of Servetus's execution. Again Servetus soliloquises, bemoaning his fate, 'The ghastly farce is over! Well I knew I was foredoomed…Calvin has won and I have lost the day!" And then he asks a question which many others have asked about him since,

> …I wonder…. Let me search my soul
> In near approach of death…. if I were he
> And he were I…. I wonder should I be
> As bent on crushing him by chains and death
> As he has been to clear me from his way!

Reassuringly, he decides,

> …. Methinks I should not be as harsh!
> My thought of God is not the same his;
> And what we think of God must shape our
>   mood
> Making us stern or gentle, like itself!

Calvin, he reflects, "has wrought a system of cold
thought…a loveless creed." But his thoughts then turn
to the terrible fate that awaits him. He has asked
Calvin to visit him, resolved to plead for his life.
Then Calvin arrives. [*Second extract,* **Scene Three:**
"Unhappy man: what wilt thou? I am here!" to, "The
world will judge betwixt us."]

~

"The Diary of Catalina Conesa," by Jane Rzepka and adapted by Polly Guild [3 readers]

The work of two contemporary Unitarian-Universalist ministers in the United States, this monologue was written for use in a worship context. It is the fictional diary of the mother of Michael Servetus, beginning in 1513 when he was two and ending on 30th October 1553, when news of his death reached her in Spain. It is, of course, entirely imaginary. However, it brings a maternal and feminine perspective to a story that is almost entirely masculine throughout! [*Extracts* as indicated.]

~

"Csillag a Máglyán [Flames at the Stake"], by Andras Sütõ. English translation by Alan Williams [2 readers and 4 readers]

This play is the work of a contemporary Hungarian playwright, and I am indebted to the British Unitarian, Alan Williams, for translating it into English. Alan makes the point that the play is really an allegory about the Cold War, Communist era of the 1970s, when it was written. Sütõ uses the story of Servetus to comment on the ideological oppression that characterised Communist-run countries such as Hungary and Romania.

Alan says of its portrayal of Servetus that he, "is presented rather like Dostoevsky's Idiot—a holy fool," and that his, "speech often seems on the edge of madness." The play does not pretend to be accurate historically, for this is not its purpose. In its story of informers, of the show trial, of the refusal to allow Servetus the right to speak, it drew attention to the audience's more immediate concerns. But then even at the time, in 1553, Servetus soon became the symbol of a much wider struggle for what later became known as 'human rights.'

Our *first extract* is from **Act II,** and is a confrontation between Calvin and Servetus, not only about points of theology, but also about the way Geneva is run under the pervasive influence of the Reformation's chief ideologue. ["We could have carried on our battle in private," to, "Or without it tripping up the person who uttered it." Edited.]

The *second extract,* with which we close, is from the play's penultimate scene. It is polyphonic. Calvin is preaching. Servetus speaks in his cell, anticipating a chance to debate publicly that will never come. Then we hear the voice of Calvin's mentor and greatest ally, Guillaume Farel. He reports the arrest of the Syndic, Perrin, and then the verdicts of the Protestant cities of Switzerland in the case of Servetus. An unidentified voice begins to speak, calling for Servetus's death. While Calvin still declaims and Servetus pleads for the chance to reply, Farel pronounces the verdict. ["Have mercy on us, O

Lord," to, "May the Lord turn his face towards you and be merciful. Amen."]

~

Painting by Theodor Pixis (1831–1907), showing an outwardly peaceful Calvin who tries to convince an irascible Servetus.

APPENDIX 1

SERVETUS: A DRAMA*

Henry Warburton Hawkes (1843–1917)

— ~ —

**[1.] From Scene II. A cell in the prison at Geneva.
Servetus in fetters. Enter Calvin.**

Cal. Servetus, know'st thou me?

Ser.   Ay! that right well,
    Though thou and I have aged since first we met,
     I stood amidst the crowd when thou didst preach
     Before they seized me prisoner. 'Twas the day
    Thou didst compel the Syndic to submit
    To thy autocracy, and I did mark
    The ring of triumph in thy voice and word.
    Dost always triumph so o'er beaten foes?

Cal. When they are foes of God and man alike,
    And I have served Him by their overthrow
    Do I not well to triumph, as He must!

* Extracts selected and edited by Clifford M. Reed.

Ser. Thou thinkest God is ever on thy side
And I must agree with what thou deemest fit?
Beyond all doubt a comforting belief.
I would that I could ever feel as sure!

Cal. Thou scoffest at me yet! I do recall
Long years ago when thou in Paris dwelt
Thou didst indite a book of heresy
Full of thy scoffing jibes and ribaldries.
Perchance thou didst not think the day would
       come
When not thy books alone, but thou thyself
Would stand condemned for rankest blasphemy!

Ser. I well recall the book, and well recall
How thou didst fail to meet my arguments
When in debate I met thee face to face.
Today thou hast an argument at hand
Of other breed. These fetters and this gaol
With God knows what beside, are reasons strong
To prove thee in the right! I would not use
Such arguments if I were in thy place,
But rather trust to brains!

Cal.   Rash fool! Beware!
I came with good intent and in the hope
That even yet thy stubborn mind would yield,
Not to my arguments, but to the Truth
Revealed in Holy Scripture. I am here
As Christ's Ambassador, to offer peace
If thou wilt now recant thy heresy.

137

Thy jeers and gibes avail not! 'Tis not me
Thou dost reject, by th' Eternal Son
Whose Godhead is the very heart of truth
Whereby mankind is saved. To know the Son
Is everlasting life: but to deny
His perfect Godhead is most certain death!
Servetus! Pause and weigh the matter well.

Ser. 'Revealed in Holy Scripture' say'st thou! Nay!
And Nay! a thousand times. I too have read
And studied Scripture from my early youth:
Yea, know it every line. I find not there
The Godhead of the Son, the Trinity,
Nor other fictions foisted on the Church!
I find One God, the Father, neither more
Nor less, one undivided unity!
I find one Christ, created within time
To work the works of God; the spoken word
Incarnate, but derived himself from God,
Not being God, but creature made by God!
This is the faith the first Apostles knew
And this the faith the written word reveals.

Cal. Rank blasphemy! I tell thee yet again
Thou dost oppose thy stubborn ignorance
Against the faith of hoar antiquity!
The Church condemned a heresy like thine
And cast it forth, long centuries ago.
What! Shall thy puny mind in vain conceit
Oppose the faith of ages. Were the saints,
The martyrs, the confessors, all the wise

And learned theologians, in the wrong
With all the myriad unnamed Christian souls,
While thou, poor empty fool, would'st set them
     right
And make pretence that thou hast found the
     Truth
Which all the rest have missed! Sure thou art
     mad,
Puffed up with empty vanity and pride,
To rank thyself against the Church of God!

Ser. And dost *thou* find this very Church of God
Agree with all that *thou* believest true?
Does Luther, that great leader of reform,
Aecolompadius, Zwingli, Melanchthon,
Erastus, all reformers good and true,
Have they seen eye to eye with thee in all
Thy scheme of doctrine? I trow not indeed!
And dost thou pit thyself against them all?
Deeming that they are wrong and thou art right.
While yet thou chargest me with vain conceit
Because I, too, see truth with mine own eyes?

Cal. I will not stay to bandy words with thee!
I see thy heart is hardened 'gainst the truth,
Thy eyes are blinded lest they see the light.
I leave thee now to justice. I have striven
To make this city, once debased and vile,
An Eden-spot of earth; but as of yore
The serpent poisoned Eden with his guile,
So thou would'st with thy heresies destroy

139

The souls of Adam's sons, regenerate,
And drag them down to hell 'long with thyself!
It shall not be! The strong arm of the law
Shall curb thy wickedness and blasphemy!
God in His mercy give thee penitence.

Exit hastily.

END SCENE II

~

[2.] From Scene III. Cell in prison as before, Servetus in fetters. 26th October 1553. Enter Calvin.

Cal.   Unhappy man: what wilt thou? I am here!

Ser. Calvin, if in thy bosom lurks one spark
Of that divinest gift of God, sweet Charity,
I do beseech thee now to pity me!
I do abase myself before thee! See
How I am humbled! If in days gone by
I have opposed thee, flouted thee with jeers,
Made merry o'er thy learned arguments,
I now repent me. Put it from thy mind
And only think of mercy!
Hast thou thought
What it would be if thou didst lie condemned
To such a fearsome death as waits for me?
Hast thou conceived the horror of the flames,
The singeing of the flesh, the blackened limbs!

And if thou hast, canst thou in sullen hate
Wish that thy bitterest foe should suffer thus!
Oh, Calvin, mercy! If thou wilt forgive
And intercede for me, thy power is great
And thou canst save me from such an awful
    doom.
If thou wilt spare me, never will I ope
My lips to speak on God's divine decrees,
Ne'er meddle with theology again,
But give my mind to usefulness of life.
I will submit to anything but this
With willing heart. Do with me what thou wilt
But save me from the flames!
               I once did hear
That thou art not as stern as thou dost seem;
That in the years gone by, thou hadst a wife
Whom thou didst love; had children born to thee
Whom thou dost mourn!
              If thou art human still,
By all these sacred memories I implore
For pity. Think of those dear angels blest
Whom thou hast loved and lost; and let the
    thought
Melt from thy heart all memories of hate
And fill it with the tenderness of Christ!
Have mercy as thou hop'st for mercy too!

Cal. Unhappy man! Repentance comes too late!
    The die is cast and cannot be recalled.
    Think not I hate thee, as thou twice hast said.
    It is not *thee* I hate. There was a time

When I perchance was angered at the gibes
With which thou didst assail all argument,
But that is past!

             In His wise providence
The Lord hath set me in a lofty place,
Though all unworthy, and has given me charge
To preach the word of righteousness and truth.
Upon a watch-tower He hath set me high,
To guard the flock from wolves and robber-
        bands!
Thou art the wolf that would devour the sheep!
Thou art the robber that would steal their souls!
I'd sooner let black plague within the fold
To ravage as it would, than suffer in
False doctrine such as thine. The plague might
        kill
The mortal bodies; but thy heresies
Poison the very springs of life and spread
Their baleful venom through the gates of death.
What are the few short pangs which in the morn
Await thy house of clay, put in compare
With all the quenchless fires of hell which wait
The unbeliever and the infidel
Who has rejected God's revealed truth!
I will not lift one finger to avert
The doom thou hast deserved. When I recall
The evil thou hast by thy teaching done,
The doubt and unbelief that thou hast bred,
Methinks the stake and faggots are too kind.

       Yet still I have some pity on thy soul.

If from thy heart thou would'st confess thy sin
And now recant thy error; publish wide
Thy condemnation of thy former ways,
And to the Church of God be reconciled,
Perchance a milder death might yet be thine!
I give thee this one chance! Wilt thou recant?

Ser. Recant! Nay, ten thousand times! Avaunt
Thou worse than Satan! Thou would'st have
     me go
Before my Maker with a deadly lie
Fresh on my tongue. Think'st thou the intellect
Can cheat itself, and for a present gain
See black as white; swing like a pendulum
From truth to error; falsify itself
With ready ease, and think it now believes
What years of earnest thought has banned as
     false.
My body shrinks from faggot and from flame.
It is a trembling coward; but my soul
Thus challenged to be true spurns with contempt
Thy sorry bribe!
           I doubt not thou would'st love
To have it blazoned to thy little world
Of sycophants, that at his latter end,
Servetus, who for years had held his own
And had opposed his arguments to thine,
Had bowed to thy superior piety
And owned thee in the right!
              I will not yield
One jot or tittle of my honest faith

At thy persuasion! Take thy triumph now
And hug it to thy breast. In years to come
The world will judge betwixt us.

END SCENE III

~

Christopher Sichem made this copper portrait of
Servetus in Holland, 1607.

APPENDIX 2

THE DIARY OF CATALINA CONESA*
The imaginary reminiscences of the mother of
Michael Servetus

Jane Rzepka
Minister, Church of the Larger Fellowship, USA

— ~ —

VILLANUEVA, HUESCA PROVINCE, SPAIN:
August 13th 1513.

It's good to be alive! Today we move to a grand new house, the most wonderful in the village—and near the parish church. Perhaps one day little Michael will be a priest there. He is just two now, and as I write is busily unpacking all that I've gathered for our trip. Antonio will hold the important office of Notary in the village.

The atmosphere in Spain today is calmer. King Ferdinand and Queen Isabella have saved the Catholic Church. Most of the Moors have been

* Adapted by Polly Guild and further adapted by Clifford Reed. Performed as a three-voice dramatic reading in Geneva, 26th October 2003.

baptised. I am sad about those who have been exiled or sent to the stake. I'm glad that Michael will never see the horrors that his father and I have seen. There can only be ONE religion, but why must religion cause so much suffering? But it's a good time to dream, a good time to raise a child.

~

June 30th 1528.

Michael is studying at the University of Toulouse, the most celebrated in all of Europe. I am so proud of him! He has learned Latin, Greek and Hebrew in addition to his studies in law. It is a good school, very orthodox, and it has many relics and images. They do not tolerate heresy.

I am worried, though. Michael is reading the Bible, a practice that is strictly forbidden. We have taken great pains to teach him right from wrong, and we have seen to it that he knows his catechism. The very best schools have taught him that God has three forms. He understands that they are all eternal. Those two doctrines are all that matters. But at sixteen he thinks he knows it all!

He is thrilled with the Bible. The book has come to him from heaven, he says. He finds it warm and inspiring. Now everybody knows that religion is not supposed to be inspiring. It is supposed to SAVE!

But there is something worse. Michael says that there is not a word about the Trinity in the Bible. He believes Christ to be a man—Jesus of Nazareth—not eternal at all. He is intensely taken with this idea. It consumes him. It isn't healthy. Our son is too young to see the dangers. How innocent he is. But will he listen to his parents?

~

March 24th 1529.

A troop of acrobats came through the village today. They told us of a glorious thing. One month a go our King Charles was crowned Holy Roman Emperor. It was magnificent and unprecedented. Princes and nobles were there from all nations, and cardinals and bishops. They said red wine spurted from the throats of the sculptured lions. Fife, drum, trumpet and trombone made it sound like Judgement Day!

The most Holy Father, Clement VII, rode in the midst of four cardinals on foot. On his head was a triple crown, and he sat in a golden chair beneath a golden canopy. When the Pope and Emperor met, His Majesty kissed the feet of His Holiness, and begged to be received as his son. If only I had been there to see it! But I mustn't complain. Michael was there and will report it all to me any day.

~

March 26th 1529.

The coronation has affected Michael badly. He saw nothing wonderful about the occasion. He claims he saw only worldliness, ambition and sacrilege. He is sick at heart.

I have lost patience with this difficult child, this schoolboy! He has been given nothing but the best and yet he is so wrong-headed. He has called the Pope a "beast of beasts most wicked". Oh, where will it end?

~

October 29th 1529.

Now Michael wants to reform us all! I suppose he has made friends with reformers, young impatient men who want to argue, who have their own ideas, who think the old ways of change are timid and lukewarm.

But even Luther and Calvin are not zealous enough for Michael. At twenty years of age he has declared to all that the Council of Nicaea was wrong, that the dogma of three eternal persons in the Godhead is mistaken. The spirit of youth is so uncompromising.

Michael is travelling now, obsessed with his mission, brazenly visiting all the leaders of the Reformation. He forces his way into their houses, these dignified preachers and professors. He becomes quite wild and insists they adopt his views. They drive him away. He is unreasonable and believes that he alone knows the truth.

Is this the way with all young people? Or is Michael possessed? Oh, how my heart aches.

~

June 3rd 1531.

I am a widow. Every now and then I catch myself, expecting to hear Antonio's step or laugh or sigh, but I hear only long empty silence. Yet there is joy for me in my son, Juan, now that he has entered the priesthood. Juan and I will erect an altarpiece to Santa Lucia in the parish church. An altarpiece is real religion, true comfort, real.

Juan understands religion. Michael does not. The boys went to the same school. I raised them the same way. Why are they so different? People say Michael as an "unsoothed itch". He has just published a book in Strasbourg. No one would listen to his views, so he printed them. He even proudly placed his name on the title page. The book is called, 'The Errors of the Trinity'. Michael has made people very angry—much to his surprise. He doesn't see that even reformers have limits.

Now that he has declared both Catholics and Protestants to be wrong, he is hunted everywhere. The Protestants say he deserves to have his guts torn out

of his living body. The Catholics have asked Juan—
his brother!—to go to Germany and lay a plot to
ensnare him.

Poor Michael must be terrified and lonely now.
He has been foolish but he meant no harm. He is only
a boy. He talks of the New World.

~

July 10ᵗʰ 1552.

It is now some twenty years since Michael
disappeared. Rumours go around that he is dead, that
he died mad in a castle dungeon. But I know better.
He lives in France and has a new name, a new life. He
never speaks of theology any more. He has finally
made his peace with the Catholic Church. He has
learned his lesson and grown up. My heart is at peace.

He is still proud, arrogant, impatient—God
forgive him! But now his arrogance doesn't put him
in so much danger. Michael has done some editing—
a new book about the geography of the New World.

He began to study medicine and has written a
popular little book on syrups. He says he has been
cutting up dead bodies. Whatever next! And he says
he knows how blood moves through the lungs.

If only he can keep his nose out of religion! He is
a very popular doctor. In fact, some of his
competition gave him a beating, they were so envious

of people's love for him. And why not? Where were
they during the plague of '42? At court or tending to
urgent country matters, while Michael made his calls
up and down the streets of Vienne. He is a good boy.

~

January 2ⁿᵈ 1553.

Yesterday the Abbot came to dinner, and Juan
with him. They brought bad news. Michael is writing
books on religion again. He has been working on
forbidden subjects all along! Perhaps it was those new
bibles he edited years ago. The Abbot said they
started him thinking again. He has been reading some
things by John Calvin and, presumptuous boy,
thought he could instruct Calvin by sending him
manuscripts of his latest work! Kindly, Calvin
replied, but Michael didn't understand the honour
done him.

Instead of being flattered the conceited fool
denounced Calvin for not admitting his errors, and
sent him another thirty manuscripts! Calvin sent
Michael a copy of his book, which Michael returned
with the margins scribbled full of sarcastic
comments! Idiot! As though he were correcting a
student's composition! Calvin called Michael's work,
"the hee-haw of a donkey".

Michael has written another book, which he
called, 'The Restoration of Christianity'. It was
printed in great secrecy. The Abbot says that he has it

on good authority that the manuscript—all seven
hundred pages—was burned leaf by leaf as the
printed pages were set in type. But my foolish son!
He put his initials at the end and his name in the text.

The Abbot says that if the Calvinists don't burn
him, the Catholics will. He attacks the most Holy
Trinity with every weapon of Satan. He is bitter about
the true Church, but even angrier with the reformers,
who don't go far enough for him. Calvin has seen the
book and he is not a patient man.

The Abbot was quiet then. Juan did not reply. I
felt his shame for his brother. But I felt a sorrow too
deep for words, a sorrow no mere brother could feel. I
made the sign of the cross and went to my room.

~

March 18th 1553.

March 18th 1553.

This morning a visiting priest said Mass. He had
been sent by the Inquisitor to explain again the
Church's mission to the world. It is of the utmost
importance that the unbelievers—Heathens, Jews and
Moors—confess the truth of the doctrines of the
Universal Church. Only in this way could they be
saved and God's Kingdom come on earth.

For the first time in many years I recalled a
Jewish servant of my neighbours'. She had accepted
baptism long before the Inquisition began, but
continued her observance of the Jewish holidays.

When the Inquisitor came to our village, she was brought before him and questioned. She was asked to declare her faith in the Holy Trinity and the Divinity of Christ Jesus, the Eternal Son of God. She could not. Three times she was pressed to answer. Three times she refused. She was taken out to the market place and burned.

All this appeared to me in an instant and I thought: "If the Church would embrace all people, why should it put such barriers in their way?" Our village had been so peaceful before the Inquisitor came. Then burnings, torture, imprisonment. We looked at each other with suspicion or shame.

The Gospel today was about the child Jesus teaching the elders in the Temple. God forgive me, I thought of Michael so many years ago, in all his rash pride, questioning his holy fathers and baiting them.

~

July 15th 1553.
Juan tells me that Michael is a renegade again. Calvin has sent the Inquisitors a copy of Michael's book. He hopes they will do what he, far away in Geneva, cannot.

The Protestants must detest their heretics as much as we do ours. Michael was warned. The presses disappeared, the printers denied all knowledge, and Michael denied that he was the Spaniard Servetus. It almost worked, until Michael wrote to Calvin again, scolding him for helping the Inquisition. Calvin just sent them more evidence. "Think of it," Juan said, "the leaders of the Reformation helping the Inquisitors to burn a heretic!"

It seems that they tricked Michael, asking him to treat some patients in the royal prison, and then made him a prisoner, too. But he escaped through the prison garden. Juan was sent the fur robe and velvet nightcap Michael left behind.

Michael was gone, but the Inquisitor went ahead with the trial anyway and Michael was found guilty of heresy. If he had not escaped he would have paid one hundred pounds to the King and he and his books would have been carted through the streets to the market place, where he would have been burned at the stake. Since he was gone, they'll have to settle for burning his effigy, along with five bales of blank paper in place of his books!

~

October 30th 1553.

October 30th 1553.
Michael is dead. Juan told me that Michael had been wandering through France these four months and had decided to flee to Naples, where many Spaniards live. But instead of travelling through Piedmont, he chose to go by way of Geneva. The fool. I was bitter with grief and anger. Juan could only shake his head.

Michael went out of his way to cause trouble. Since it was Sunday when he arrived, he went to church. He was recognised. Though Michael had not broken any of Geneva's laws, he was arrested and imprisoned. There was a trial. Michael, of course, was insolent. He denied the Trinity and the eternal Divinity of Christ. He even rejected infant baptism, calling it an invention of the Devil!

He accused Calvin of trying to bring about his death in France. He was so abusive and shameless that the judges were disgusted at his excesses. Michael refused to listen to reason and thought his case as good as won.

After weeks in prison, gnawed at by rats and without a single change of clothes, he was found guilty of heresy and sentenced to death. They encouraged him to recant. He would not. Even the slightest show of modesty would have given them an excuse to spare his life.

Michael was burned with his books. A dreamer, an exasperating dreamer! My son was drawn to trouble, but he loved Jesus devotedly and cherished the Bible far above all other books. May God have mercy on his soul.

~

"Servetus in the jail of Geneva," drawing by Pablo Ruíz Picasso, 1904, in the National Library of Madrid.

APPENDIX 3

CSILLAG A MÁGLYÁN
[Flames at the Stake*]

Andras Sütõ

— ~ —

**[1.] From Act II. The scene is the Geneva
Consistory Council room, campaign headquarters
of the Reformation.**

Servetus: We could have carried on our battle in
   private—in perfect freedom and safety—God
   would have allowed it. Except that my letters
   found their way to the Inquisition in Paris. This is
   all that Michael Servetus, alias Villanovanus,
   wishes to say to the head of the Reformation, to
   the sometime Lucanius. *(Hesitatingly makes for
   the door.)* I dared debate with you, my words
   were of good bread—and you could have returned
   them with mud or stones—but to inform on me!

Calvin: You think I informed on you?

*** English translation © by Alan Williams. Extracts selected
and edited by Clifford Reed for a dramatic reading in Geneva.**

Servetus: I saw with my own eyes the report on the Inquisitor's desk. My ideas, shared only with you.

Calvin: Your attacks on Christ's divinity, on salvation through faith, on predestination, on baptism. All degenerated into a mad howling inside you, Michael.

Servetus: I have a passionate nature. I am the victim of the Inquisition, not its ally.

Calvin: It was Farel who sent your letters to the Inquisition without my knowledge. Listen to me Michael, I may strike you down, or you may sweep all this away, but I will never lie to you.

Servetus *(joyfully):* Lucanius! Now I am hearing your old voice! Don't be angry at me for doubting your words. I came to rid myself of this very doubt.

Calvin: And the rest of your doubts?

Servetus: I don't know. I fled here, like you, dressed as a grape-picker with his pitcher, out of the arms of the Inquisition. I've been hiding these four months—in Europe! The birthplace of humanism!

Calvin: You shouldn't have come here.

Servetus: Should I have gone to Rome? To my

enemies? *(Searching in his bundle.)* I wanted personally to give you my latest book. My little book, to the author of the *Institutio Christianismi.* Take it with my love—the *Restitutio.*

Calvin: Put it away. It's for the flames.

Servetus: The book? My writing?

Calvin: Your errors.

Servetus: You call it error to oppose your ideas, or even to diverge from them a little?

Calvin: It is heresy.

Servetus: But you yourself are a heretic, cursed by the Pope. You may not speak like this, because of your... triumph. Your bailiffs defend your teachings.

Calvin: I am obliged to speak thus, because of your errors as well. I have not triumphed. At any moment the Libertines could deliver Geneva into the arms of the French, and then it would not be the poorer by your book, but by several thousand lives. Put away your book and go in peace. You've come to a bad place—this isn't Arcadia. Here are no walkways for Greek philosophers. Instead, like a child, you've stumbled on to a battleground. I don't ask you to stand with us. For

17 years we have debated without result. I can't expect you to put down your weapons and take up ours. Only ultimate mercy can absolve you of the sin of denying the Trinity. Leave this place that I am forced to live in. I too desire solitude and study. I too am repelled by war, but here in Geneva is the only way that leads to God. Even if God has led me here to break me, it makes my conscience stronger, since I know it is His will.

Servetus: And what if He has led me here too?

Calvin: Then His plan is to ruin my work of decades, and that of Luther too, and to stand you in our place. To reform the Reformation, when we are hardly even begun.

Servetus: I am not your enemy.

Calvin: It is not your intention to be.

Servetus: Is that not enough?

Calvin: A well-intentioned candle in the hands of a child. Let us leave this question of your intentions. They've been proved wrong. Where were you travelling?

Servetus: I don't know myself. I came to you. I want to go on to Zurich from here, and then to Naples. A friend is preaching there.

Calvin: Another antitrinitarian?

Servetus: There are enough of those here.

Calvin: Please God it was not them who invited you here.

Servetus: I know nothing of them, I swear it.

Calvin: You swear too easily. Here you are, sleepwalking around Europe. Again, I ask, do you know where you have come? The city is full of Libertines and sectarians. Through your book you have become like them.

Servetus: But I don't want to organise a party against you in this city.

Calvin: Since Gutenberg, such battles have been fought with armies of lead. And don't leave your books here in place of yourself.

Servetus: You're not going to burn them at the stake, are you? *(Laughs.)*

Calvin: Yes. In Geneva, only one book is permitted: the Holy Book.

Servetus: So no democracy—instead, a bibliocracy. Of course, your books are permitted too.

Calvin: They do not deny the divinity of Christ.

Servetus: Tell me, do you ever go to alehouses?

Calvin: I didn't come here to waste my time in boozing, but to create order.

Servetus: Before I go, let me tell you what I found out in them.

Calvin: I'm not interested.

Servetus: They are organising against you.

Calvin: I know all that. They have chased me out before, and then called me back—the same ones who wanted to string me up.

Servetus: This is different. Someone is working quietly and persistently against you.

Calvin: I'm listening.

Servetus: You've laid down the new rules for life in 21 articles and a catechism—and these the congregation has to accept. Anyone who offends ends up in gaol. In your city, your New Jerusalem, the most common word is, "Forbidden." Bright clothes are forbidden. On girls, silk and satin are forbidden; even new fashions are forbidden. White wine that is stronger than red is forbidden!

It is forbidden for young people to dally in secret places. It is forbidden to give newborn babies names that are not in the Bible. It is forbidden to be clean-shaven, and anyone who has any sense and enough growth wears a Calvin beard! It's forbidden to carry an unexplained package in an inn, to forward an unexamined letter anywhere. And most of all it's forbidden to discuss church matters anywhere but the Church Council.

Calvin: Go on.

Servetus: The second most common word is, "mandatory." It is mandatory for everyone to watch everyone else, to see if they are keeping the laws. It is mandatory for everyone to report everyone else they see, if they think... that is, it's not mandatory to think like this, one must do so in spite of one's conviction otherwise.

Calvin: Continue, continue—you begin to show the white of your teeth.

Servetus: I heard this too. If you don't think you should report one's fellow, you're thinking— acting— against the Consistory. And it's not just good and bad thoughts that count; it's the feelings that shine out of your face that can betray you.

During a christening, someone smiles in church— three days in prison; smile back, the Consistory. Someone else falls asleep during the

sermon and wakes up in gaol. Someone praises
the Bible translation of your persecuted enemy,
Castellio: he is persecuted too. Another calls you
a hypocrite, and he is executed. A certain
business-man by the name of Ameaux dared to
say that it wasn't even allowed to sneeze in the
Council without your permission: he had to crawl
across the main square in a scapegoat's shirt,
asking forgiveness for his opinion. 'If there's a
God, let him pay for my wine,' said a drunken
man to himself. He got six months in gaol to
sober up. Three innocent children fooling around
with each other on the riverbank after swimming;
the sentence: burning at the stake—albeit they
only showed them the fire to scare them. A satire
appears in Savoy dialect about Calvin—Jacques
Gruet is beheaded. The proof? He is the only
Savoyard in Geneva.

The total: in five years, for diverse
transgressions, there have been 77 exiled, 13
hangings, ten beheadings and 35 burnings at the
stake.

Calvin: They count well in the alehouses.

Servetus: Who decided these sentences? In whose
name?

Calvin: We were forced to—in the name of the
Reformation. We have to defend ourselves.

Servetus: Against children?

Calvin: Against armed insurrectionists.

Servetus: Against people smiling during a christening?

Calvin: You've merely gathered together those times Farel has gone too far. Your drunken friends can see no further than the end of their nose—or perhaps the bottom of the glass. I'll tell you the truth: we are at war. A religious war is beginning, and God alone knows what the end will be. But whatever it will be, Michael Servetus, I tell you they will not break Geneva—only over our bones. If the Papists or the Libertines come back here, if Zurich, Basel and Schaffhausen are lost, then we will start again in Wittenberg. If there is no godly life, no humility in this city....

Servetus: And gagged mouths, censorship of letters, mandatory uniformity of faith to the last button...

Calvin: To the last button, yes! Because in doubt, in dissolute thoughts, not only is it impossible to pray, it is impossible to work too!

Servetus: Dissolute thoughts! "I am stuck in the mire of papist idolatry," is that not what the young Calvin said to his schoolmate, Servetus, once upon a time? Have you burnt your memory of this?

Calvin: Yes, in my heart I have burnt at the stake the erring youth I once was—only for him to be resurrected at every turn in you. We come, every one, from slime and ignorance, but once we find the truth there is no more room for doubt, or we belong to the Devil.

Servetus: Or to the gallows.

Calvin: "Who would follow me must deny himself."

Servetus: Jesus did not say that in your name.

Calvin: But I say it in his, whose divinity you question.

Servetus: I simply have a different explanation. Your teaching on the Trinity was taken by Luther from Rome.

Calvin: I have no teachings. I am merely the footstool on which the Gospel rests.

Servetus: A spiked footstool!

Calvin: Because of the cross I bear and the persecution of my church.

Servetus: And as persecuted—you are becoming a

persecutor yourself. Under the name of free inquiry you are creating a religion of enforced belief, and believers you are grinding into dissemblers. All your house-searches are achieving is to multiply the numbers of hypocrites. You can't search inside the heart and inside the skull.

Calvin: I dispute that. Better to have a religion of enforced belief than a religion of false belief.

Servetus: It is your conviction—according to your commentary on Jesus—that all humanity, like some figure in a glacier, are frozen until the day of resurrection? You think you are the last thinker on earth who had the right to alter the interpretation of the Scriptures? That God created us in His own image simply so that we dully follow the same furrow for all eternity?

Calvin: Every innovation can have its influence.

Servetus: Until now, but no further. But it's such folly. It's impossible to order someone to believe, or try to force someone to believe one thing or another. Where does this futile attempt to control such secret things as inner conviction come from? How dare you even attempt it? The only result of such violent attempts is lies and play-acting. My thoughts, John, are not subject to any customs regulations.

Calvin: As Martin Luther said. Oh, Luther, rise up from your grave and listen to your own words with their original meaning turned upside down and used against you! The freedom of the Gospel, well, that has degenerated into freedom for every Anabaptist, pantheist or atheist who comes along. It is the foot-and-mouth disease of the spirit, the plague of religion, a French venereal disease sent in the form of articles that are not subject to customs regulations! Is there a woman more corrupt than the word which gives itself to any anarchist? Should pearls be cast before swine? Can a single conjunction be uttered without it being twisted into falsehood by your kind?

Servetus: Or without tripping up the person who uttered it!

[END FIRST EXTRACT]

~

[2.] From the penultimate scene. The play now becomes polyphonic. The three voices are: Calvin, preaching a sermon; Farel, speaking to the ministers and City Council; Servetus, shouting from his cell. (*Note:* Guillaume Farel had been responsible for Calvin settling in Geneva and was one of the city's senior ministers.)

Calvin (in the pulpit): Have mercy on us, O Lord, as

we give ourselves unto you. Let not our service to you be infected by our own thoughts, and let us remain unquestioningly in your will. Amen.

Servetus *(in a prison cell):* Guard! It's past eleven!

Calvin: Dearly beloved, brothers and sisters in the Lord! We have difficult times ahead of us. Once more we must confront the enemies of the Reformation. At this moment in Lyon, our young brothers in faith are stepping towards the stake with the words of the 9th Psalm on their lips, while the Emperor Charles is sending his Spanish vassals against Geneva to bring us under the yoke of Rome. And a mere pistol shot from our borders, Bishop de la Beaume is preparing mass-murder for us—at this moment.

Remember my vigilance over you all, men and women, young and old, the poor and the wealthy. We will all die if we do not stand united. This city, once a nest of idolaters, a new Sodom and Gomorrah, has become, in 15 years of war and struggle, like unto the city of God. We have given our blood in sacrifice for it—the beloved martyrs of the pure Gospel have had their tongues pierced, and have chosen the scaffold rather than say the Ave Maria once more.

Servetus: Guard! I want to speak to the prison governor!

Calvin: Our sacrifice has borne fruit. When God looks on us he is filled with joy. You know, brothers and sisters, that I do not intend praise for myself nor glory in my own acts. It is such a joy to see the changes of the past days—and that others say so. Here is Vergerius, former papist Bishop of Istria, forced to this opinion of us *(reads)*:

> "What a congregation is to be seen in Geneva! When the bells sound, the traders close up their shops and stop work, and make for the nearest church to sing the Psalms of David and to hear the Holy Word..."

Servetus: Guard! I must speak in church! Don't you understand? Don't you hear me, you dog? I'll report you, you villain!

Calvin: "...Let us praise God in our own tongue, without the obscuring medium of Latin, in freedom and openness..."

Servetus: Send a message to Calvin, faithless scoundrel!

Farel *(in the Council room):* I pray you, hear the decision of the city Security Council in the case of Monsieur Perrin. In order to defend the security of the city in our threatened state, he has been arrested and is hereby detained.

Calvin: "…Geneva, blessed city, within whose walls Paganism is done away with! Blessed city, which has brought the light of free inquiry for the first time in a thousand years!"

Thus the letter, after which I ask: where are you, Michael Servetus, foul monster of heresy, destroyer of our peace, our unity, with your Anabaptism, pantheism and stinking antitrinitarianism? Stand out here in front of all, so that I might answer your blasphemous questions. Show yourself to the congregation, so they can see the face of him, who dashed down the Pope but failed to raise up Christ in his place, who denied Christ's divinity in the obscenity of his book, *Christianismi Restitutio.*

A Voice: Where is he? Let us see him!

Calvin: Alas, you will see him. He will be here soon.

Servetus: Guard! Warder! State Secretary! Prison Governor! Where are you, Calvin? Your actions prove you a coward and a murderer! You don't dare engage in open debate! I have no fear of death, as my case is just. In vain do you cry out against me, like a blind man in an empty desert.

Farel (*counting the votes of the Swiss cantons*): Basel: against. Zurich: against. Schaffhausen: against—and they add the comment, "Deliver us

171

from this foul heretic."

Calvin: Against his empty questions every upright
Christian revolts. His first question: "Was the
crucified man, Jesus, the son of God, and if so,
why?" Do you hear? *Why?* His second question:
"Is the city of God within people, and if so, when
will it be reached, when will they be born again?"
Do you hear? "When will they be born again?" I
tell you: when the Church is rid of you and people
like you!

Servetus: You twist my every word, as the spirit of
revenge is burning up your heart, and you lie, lie,
you ignorant slanderer! At the slightest opposition, rage fills you up—even about such things as
the weather! Where are you God, where are you
Christ, when the innocent are condemned to death
in your name?

Farel *(dictating):* The case brought by Nicolas de la
Fontaine against Michael Servetus of Villanova in
the Kingdom of Aragon, has been heard by the
Council of Judges on this day, October 26th, in
the year of Our Lord 1553. The accused has
admitted every point of the prosecution's case.
His heretical books, printed and distributed in
secret, have horrified and disgusted Geneva's
Church Council and those of its sister-cities
alike…

Calvin: Third question: "Is faith necessary for baptism, and what is the purpose of the sacraments in the New Testament?" Are you listening? "Is faith necessary for baptism?" Himself denying the right of children to be baptised, he had himself baptised anew at the age of thirty! Imagine it—as the bearded 'infant' is held under the holy water by Satan himself as godfather, and as godmother, some hideous female devil!

Servetus: Just give me a chance, give me the opportunity to deny these terrible lies! Book burning is not the answer! Not to anything! Putting someone to death is not the same as winning the argument! Convince me I'm wrong in my beliefs. Don't convict me, convince me, for pity's sake! Will the heavens not split above you when you turn personal enmity into heresy?

Calvin: His fourth question: "And what if all those sacraments in the New Testament are allegorical?" Allegorical—and thus meaningless, empty papist ceremonies.

A Voice: To the fire with him!

Calvin: And his fifth question: "Where is the mercy in Jesus' coming? And before he came, were all of our forefathers condemned to hell?" Such a low, sneaking question, like a snake in the grass!

The whore of Babylon hides in this nest of doubts, masquerading as 'free thought.' This 'freethinker' has given himself like a low prostitute to every passing fancy, a true representative of Dante's Hell—a space, emptiness, a great nothing. But emptiness is dangerous to the blind in faith. His emptiness is damaging to every Christian whose faith is undermined by doubt. To lead him away from such error is impossible now—to attempt to do so would lead to our destruction.

A Voice: To the scaffold with him!

Servetus: You have grown fat on condemnation, and made the truth what you will. Why does no arrow of God strike you down? Who gave you ownership over me? Did you buy me as a slave from my mother and father? I was a born thinker, not a slave-master. I need the freedom to act, not just with my body, but with my mind as well.

Where are you Calvin, God of all the answers? Where is the man who will submit to the slavery of another's beliefs, who will condemn himself to hypocrisy in the name of another's 'freedom'? Let the apostle Paul be my defender; let him be a slave to his own conscience. Convince me, convince me if I'm wrong!

Farel: We, the city fathers and prosecuting judges, on the basis of the trial now completed, being convinced that in spite of every warning and admonishment, you continue to promulgate your heretical teachings, you continue to work against the basis of our Christian faith, you have caused split and dissent within our church, and you have shamelessly spread your doctrines throughout the world...

Servetus: Do you think I have no arguments? Polycarpus, Keleman, Tertullian...

Calvin: Not even Polycarpus said such a thing! Cyprian states the opposite. The doctrine of the Trinity has been accepted since before the Nicaean synod!

Servetus: Where are you Aristotle? Show them the truth! Plato is dear to me, but the truth is still dearer—my sufferings are my truth. Oh my dear mother! Why did you bring me into such a cruel world?

Calvin: But what need is there for all this, when he himself admits his actions?

A Voice: Let him admit them! Bring him before us!

Calvin: He would admit them if he had not fled from open debate. You are trapped for a second time, Michael Servetus—for the second and last time. May the Lord turn his face toward you and be merciful. Amen.

[END SECOND EXTRACT]

~

A Martyr Soul Remembered:
Commemorating the 450th Anniversary of the
Death of Michael Servetus

DAY IV

Monday, 27th October 2003

— ~ —

MORNING: Champel

The International Council of
Unitarians & Universalists

A SERVICE

TO COMMEMORATE

THE 450th ANNIVERSARY OF

THE MARTYRDOM OF

MICHAEL SERVETUS (1511–1553)
THEOLOGIAN and PHYSICIAN

HELD AT

CHAMPEL, GENEVA

27th OCTOBER 2003

OPENING WORDS, "Flame of the Spirit," spoken by Cynthia Cain and written by Clifford M. Reed:

Flame of the Spirit, blazing in the wind of
  Pentecost.
Flame of the martyrs' witness, blowing in the
  gales of history.
Flame of our liberal faith, rising from the
  crescent earth to celebrate our blue planet
  and its web of life.

Chalice of humanity, calling all to share
  God's grace and bounty with justice
  and equality.
Chalice of the common cup, welcoming without
  condition all who come to worship
  in goodwill.
Chalice of our world community, from which
  we drink the wine of love to make us
  one in freedom.

INVOCATION, by Clifford M. Reed:

As representatives of the worldwide community
of Unitarians and Universalists we are gathered
here in Champel, "about a musket shot from
Geneva," as an earlier pilgrim described it. In this
place, 450 years ago today, Michael Servetus was
cruelly and unjustly put to death by burning. His
achievements were many, but we see in him a
pioneer of our movement of the free and loving

Spirit. And, though thought and theology may change, the path of questing faith that he followed and the way of love to which he aspired, continue to enhance and redeem the human race. What killed Servetus here on that dark day was our all-too-human fear and arrogance, our cold hearts and our closed minds. May those who killed him be forgiven. May we be saved from the errors into which they fell—and which blight the world still. And may, "Jesus, Son of the Eternal God, have pity," on us all.

SONG, "Gathered Here," words and music by Philip A. Porter, in *Singing the Living Tradition,* Beacon Press, no. 389.

READINGS, read by Christine Hayhurst and Andrew M. Hill:
from **The Gospel of Thomas, v.77, translated by Thomas O. Lambdin.**
Jesus said, "It is I who am the light which is above them all. It is I who am the All. From Me did the All come forth, and unto Me did the All extend. Split a piece of wood, and I am there. Lift up the stone and you will find Me there."

from **The Acts of the Apostles, ch.7:48–60, translated by William Tyndale, 1534.**

Howbeit he that is highest of all, dwelleth not in temples made with hands; as saith the prophet: Heaven is my seat, and earth is my footstool, what house will ye build for me saith the Lord? Or what place is it that I should rest in? hath not my hands made all these things? Ye stiffnecked and of uncircumcised hearts and ears: ye have always resisted the holy ghost: as your fathers did, so do ye. Which of the prophets have not your fathers persecuted? And they have slain them, which shewed before of the coming of that just, whom ye have now betrayed and murdered...When they heard these things, their hearts clave asunder and they gnashed on him with their teeth. But he being full of the holy ghost, looked up steadfastly with his eyes into heaven...and said: behold, I see the heavens open and the son of man standing on the right hand of God. Then they gave a shout...and ran upon him all at once, and cast him out of the city and stoned him...And he kneeled down and cried with a loud voice: Lord lay not this sin to their charge. And when he had thus spoken, he fell asleep.

RESPONSIVE READING. "Not out of hell: responding to Servetus," based on words by Michael Servetus in his *Christianismi Restitutio,* 1553. Led by Christine Hayhurst:

"Not out of hell shall we rise,"
save that of our own making;

"Nor future judgment shall we dread,"
save that of our own conscience;

"Gifted already with eternal life,"
as we are if we did but know it;

"To which might Jesus, Son of the Eternal God,
    conduct us all,"
as we become aware of his Spirit's leading;

"For he is of this eternal life author and finisher,"
the Divine within ourselves and all creation.

**READING, "Remembering," written and read
    by Celia Midgley, Geneva 26th–27th
    October 2003:**
It is the decent thing we do now
the proper rite for one who mattered
whose death has touched us all.

Drawn by our common purpose
we offer our shame and sorrow
that death can not repair.
And now it seems we come
to kill again with kindness
to make a healing here.

We tell once more the story
we hear the cry, the pain.
We will that we remember.

And all our deaths are shared now
our lives that shout their love
our hopes that wait in ashes.

STATEMENT IN THEIR OWN LANGUAGES BY REPRESENTATIVES OF THE UNITARIAN AND UNITARIAN UNIVERSALIST MOVEMENTS:

"On behalf of *[name of church or organisation*]*
I pay solemn and grateful tribute to Michael
Servetus, martyr for his faith and for the rights of
conscience which we uphold."

* Deutsche Unitaria Religionsgemeinschaft represented by
Manfred Paul; European Unitarian Universalists, Orloff
Miller; General Assembly of Unitarians and Free Christian
Churches (UK), Barbara Smith; Unitarian Church of
Hungary, István Miko; Unitarian Church of Romania
(Transylvania), Abigel Kiss; Unitarian Universalist
Association (USA), Linda Bunyan; Unitarian /
Universalist groups not represented in person, Antje Paul,
ICUU Executive Committee.

PRAYER, "In This Season," inspired by the life and thought of Michael Servetus. Led by Cynthia Cain:

In this season of the fall,
we remember the true martyrs of our faith—and
   all faiths.

To the cross and the stake, the dungeon and the
   gas chamber;
to death by club and axe and bullet they went;
and with them went the One God,
fully present in all their human suffering,
fully present in all their human courage and
   integrity,
fully present in the love that binds us to them,
fully present in the process that brought us all out
   of nothingness.

O God who lives and makes us live,
who is the Spirit of all who live and die
   for human good,
may we know that you are One and we are
   One in you.
Amen.

*SILENT WALK DOWN THE RUE MICHEL-
   SERVET TO THE SERVETUS
   MEMORIAL*

SONG, "Gathered Here."

GREETING AND SHORT ADDRESS, by the Right Reverend Joel Stroudinsky, President of the Protestant Church in Geneva and President of the Conference of Protestant Churches of Latin European Countries.
(Also present from the Protestant Church of Geneva were Mme. Marianne Wanstall, Présidente de Région, and Pasteur Marie-Laure Jakubec of the Paroisse de Champel-Malagnou.)

WREATH LAYING, by Christine Hayhurst of the ICUU Executive Committee, *and* *SILENCE.*

CLOSING WORDS, by Michael Servetus and spoken by Clifford M. Reed:
Not out of hell shall we rise; nor future judgement shall we dread; gifted already with eternal life. To which might our most clement Lord Christ, Jesus, Son of God, conduct us all, for he is of this eternal life author and finisher.

DISMISSAL, spoken by Christine Hayhurst:
As the flame is extinguished, the spirit rises; let us go from here in peace and love. May it be so.

~

SOURCES OF THE READINGS

ROBINSON, James M., ed. *The Nag Hammadi Library in English,* 2nd edition. E.J. Brill, 1984.

TYNDALE, William, 1534. *Tyndale's New Testament: translated from the Greek.* In a modern spelling edition and with an introduction by David DANIELL. Yale University Press, 1989.

~

The Sentence Pronounced by the
SYNDICS, JUDGES of CRIMINAL CAUSES in THIS CITY

27th October 1553

— ~ —

"Thou Servetus, hast long ago put forth a false and heretical doctrine; and that slighting all remonstrances and reproofs thou hast, with a malicious and wicked obstinacy, continued to spread and publish it, so far as to print books against God the Father, the Son and the Holy Ghost; in short against the true foundation of the Christian religion, endeavouring to cause a disturbance in the church of God, whereby many souls might have been destroyed and undone (a thing horrid and dreadful, scandalous and infecting) and that thou hast not been ashamed, not afraid of rising up against the divine Majesty, and the Holy Trinity, doing thy utmost endeavours to infect the world with thy heresies and stinking heretical poison. For these causes…we condemn thee Michael Servetus to be bound, and carried to the place called Champel, and there to be fastened to a post, and burnt alive with thy books, both written with thy own hand and printed, till thy body be reduced to ashes; and thus thou shalt end thy days, to give an example to others, who would do the like.…"

A Martyr Soul Remembered:
Commemorating the 450th Anniversary of the
Death of Michael Servetus

ADDITIONAL MATERIALS

— ~ —

MICHAEL'S MEDITATIONS: Prayers and meditations
based on, inspired by or drawn from the writings
of Michael Servetus

A HYMN FOR MICHAEL SERVETUS

LIST OF CONFERENCE ATTENDEES

INTERNATIONAL COUNCIL OF UNITARIANS
AND UNIVERSALISTS

APPENDIX 4

MICHAEL'S MEDITATIONS:
Prayers and Meditations
based on, inspired by or drawn from
the writings of Michael Servetus (1511–1553)

*Written during preparation
for the Geneva commemoration by
Clifford M. Reed*

— ~ —

*"At no time can you say, 'The world is this; for before
you have finished saying it, the world has changed.'"*
— Michael Servetus, in
Christianismi Restitutio, 1553

*"Champel, or Champey, a small eminence, about a
musket shot from Geneva, was then the common place
of execution; I had the curiosity to visit the spot,
hardly known to any traveller, and to see the very
ground on which Servetus expired in flames...
This was indeed a cruel act; and in the opinion of all
good men, directly repugnant to the gentle and
humble spirit of Christ, but perfectly agreeable to the*

temper of such who are for drawing down Bonargean fire from heaven."

— Sir Benjamin Hodges, in
An Impartial History of Michael Servetus, 1724,
incorporating Lubienjecius',
Historia Reformationis Polonicae,
Book 2, Chapter 5, 1685

~

PRIMAL LIGHT
A chalice-lighting

We kindle this light,
symbol of the essential and primal light
that shone forth from the person of Jesus,
and those of all true messengers,
to flood our souls with God.

THE DIVINE IMMANENCE

O God, who we see in the true saints and great souls
    of humankind,
whose Spirit burned in Jesus as in a lantern to show
    us the way,
help us to know that you are present everywhere
    in your creation.

In the very fruits of the earth, in the animals; in stones
    and pearls
and metals and all treasures, you are there.

You are in the showers and the clouds, in the thunder
and the lightning, in the winds and the sunshine.

In the lion and the eagle, in the turtle and the dove,
in the calf and the lamb and in all that lives,
you are there.

In people as they live and die, work and dance,
    sing and pray, rejoice and grieve.

In all you are there and always were, and—
as we came to see—in him who showed to us
your boundless love.

BLOOD AND SPIRIT

Breath of God,
Which we have breathed since the moment
    of our birth
and will breathe until the moment of our death,
we rest in quietness to feel your entry and your exit.

You bring us life,
entering our lungs, entering our blood; carried round
    our bodies, through our hearts, as they toil without
    ceasing.
We rest in quietness to feel the circulation
    of the blood.

Spirit of God,
coursing through our veins almost since the moment
    of conception,
enlivening our bodies and our souls and making us
    divine, open our
minds to your presence and our hearts to your love.

DIVINE UNITY

O Thou,
whose oneness includes and embraces all
that has been made and has come to be.

O Thou,
in whom all things are present and
who is present in all things.

O Thou,
in whom there is no division, a Divine Unity
whose expression in humanity found focus
and symbol in Jesus, our brother;

Help us to know what it is to be God's child,
and so be fit vessels of your universal presence.

THE UNIVERSAL CONSCIENCE

Whatever our quality of faith concerning God,
whatever name we use to praise the Ultimate,
whatever sacred way we claim to take,
whatever sage or prophet we invoke,
whatever avatar or epiphany we say
    commands our heart,
it will suffice—if we act rightly
    according to conscience.

At the last, may the testimony of conscience alone
witness to a life that healed and blessed the world
as best it could. And in that may we be granted peace.

IN THIS SEASON

In this season of the fall,
we remember the true martyrs of our faith—
    and all faiths.

To the cross and the stake, the dungeon and
    the gas chamber;
to death by club and axe and bullet they went;
and with them went the One God,
fully present in all their human suffering,
fully present in all their human courage and integrity,
fully present in the love that binds us to them,
fully present in the process that brought us all
    out of nothingness.

O God who lives and makes us live,
who is the Spirit of all who live and die
    for human good,
may we know that you are One and we are
    One in you.
Amen.

NOT OUT OF HELL:
RESPONDING TO SERVETUS

"Not out of hell shall we rise; nor future
judgement shall we dread; gifted already with
eternal life. To which might our most clement
Lord Christ, Jesus, Son of God, conduct us all, for
he is, of this eternal life author and finisher."
— Michael Servetus, in
Christianismi Restitutio, 1553

"O Jesus, Son of the Eternal God, have pity on me."
— Michael Servetus, at
Champel, 27th October 1553

"Not out of hell shall we rise,"
save that of our own making;

"Nor future judgement shall we dread,"
save that of our own conscience;

"Gifted already with eternal life,"
as we are, if we did but know it;

"To which might Jesus, Son of the Eternal God,
conduct us all,"
as we become aware of his Spirit's leading;

"For he is of this eternal life author and finisher,"
the Divine within ourselves and all creation.

ONE GOD

O God,
you come to us in all the multifarious wonders
    of Nature,
yet you are One God.

O God,
you come to us in the infinite personalities
    of our one humanity,
yet you are One God.

O God,
you come to us in all the myriad promptings
    of love, all the
outpourings of creativity, all the strivings
    for one global commonwealth,
yet you are One God.

O God,
you come to us in all the great souls of our kind,
    in all who
have received your divine anointing inwardly done,
    and so
borne true witness to your Spirit,
yet you are One God.

...continues next page

O God,
you come to us in the fellowship and compassion
    that makes
of our variety one body, for you are One God,
    known and active
in so many ways, the binding, breathing Oneness
    of your creation.

FEELING THE HEAT
at the Michael Servetus memorial,
Geneva, 12th August 2003

On a burning August day in Geneva,
in Champel, where Rosarie meets Beau-Séjour,
I felt the heat as I looked up at a hillside memorial,
thinking of him who felt a heat much greater,
who was burned here for his faith
and for my liberty to think and write and worship
as the Spirit leads.

May I be worthy of his sacrifice.

FORGIVING CALVIN
and remembering Servetus

Can we forgive
his pride and his hardened heart
his betrayal of the way of Jesus?

Can we forgive
his bigoted hypocrisy
his theology of darkness and despair?

Can we forgive
him the pyre at Champel?

He judged another man's soul but we must not,
so we, who didn't know the secrets of his heart,
forgive him—and pray that God does too.

ALL THE WORKS OF THE LORD

"All the works of the Lord bless the one God."
— Michael Servetus, in
On the Errors of the Trinity, 1531

"For our soul is a certain light of God, a spark of the spirit of God, having an innate light of divinity."
— Michael Servetus, in
Christianismi Restitutio, 1553

All the works of the Lord bless the one God,
and praise rises from the beasts of the field and
the birds of the air; all that crawls on the earth
and swims in the waters.

All the works of the Lord bless the one God,
and prayers rise from Christian, Jew and Muslim;
acceptable are the devotions of all who worship
in love and humility.

All the works of the Lord bless the one God,
known to us in so many forms, so many dispositions.
We too are members and sharers in the Divine Unity,
called to be temples and instruments of the one Spirit.

And so we pray
that the spark and light of God will glow
brightly in our souls and in our lives.

ON TOLERANCE

"I consider it a very serious matter to kill a man
simply because he may be mistaken in some
question of interpretation of the scripture,
knowing that even the most knowledgeable ones
may fall into error."

— Michael Servetus, in a letter

Let us never kill someone
because we think them mistaken.

Let us never imprison or torture someone
because of a difference of opinion or interpretation.

Let us not even abuse or censure someone or
    impugn their character
because we think they have fallen into error.

We are so often mistaken, our own interpretation is
    so often flawed, we are so often
wrong about so many things.

Spirit of Humility,
save us from arrogance and spiritual pride,
save us from having a closed and bigoted mind.

Save us from mistaking our own malice for
    the will of God.
Remind us that the deepest evil
    is that which supposes itself virtuous.

TO A HERESY-HUNTER

"It is an heretic that makes the fire,
Not she which burns in it."

— William Shakespeare, in
The Winter's Tale, II.3

You called him 'heretic'
and made the fire that burned him.
Not with your hands, perhaps,
but with your words and imprecations.

And yet you worshipped God,
whose other name is Love.
You said you followed One for whom that Love
meant mercy, pity, peace.

You called him 'heretic'
because he spoke the truth as heart and scripture
taught him;
you whose certainty could show no mercy
though your faith required it.

I ask you now,
in love,
with all the centuries gone,
whose was the greater heresy?

DISMISSAL

As the flame is extinguished, the spirit rises;
let us go from here in peace and love.
May it be so!

~

APPENDIX 5

A HYMN FOR MICHAEL SERVETUS*

Andrew M. Hill

— ~ —

Praise God for Michael, honoured child of Spain:
  land of sunshine; also land of pain.
Jews, Moors and Christians trying to be one
  but three-fold dogma means it can't be done.
Praise God for Michael, honoured child of Spain.

Praise God for Michael, true Renaissance man,
  who first describes the Holy Spirit's plan
    as like a body circulates its blood
    so light from Christ disperses in a flood.
Praise God for Michael, true Renaissance man.

Praise God for Michael, scholar of the page,
  student of languages from every age,
who reads his Bible searching for the Three
  but what he finds is damned with heresy.
Praise God for Michael, scholar of the page.

** Written in October 2003, and set to the Genevan Psalm tune,
"Old 124th".*

Praise God for Michael, brazen, wild and bold;
enters Geneva and the tyrant's fold
where he is captured and condemned to burn:
making a lesson for the world to learn.
Praise God for Michael, brazen, wild and bold.

"Sweet Jesus, mercy: God Eternal's son."
People still struggle, freedom's scarcely won.
May we who honour Michael and his kind
still work to free the body and the mind.
"Sweet Jesus, mercy: God Eternal's son."

~

Note: The first (and last) line in the final stanza is an adaptation of Servetus' alleged last words before being burned at the stake on 27th October 1553: *"Jesus, son of the Eternal God, have mercy on me."* Had he said, "Jesus, Eternal Son of God," he would have been saved from the fire.

APPENDIX 6

CONFERENCE ATTENDEES

— ~ —

Joyce Ashworth, UK
Mary Berdjis, SW
Rev Johanna Boeke, UK
Rev Richard Boeke, UK
Linda Bunyan, USA
Rev Cynthia Cain, USA
Rev Austin Fitzpatrick, UK
Andrew Gibbs, UK
Carol Gibbs, UK
Margaret Goodwin, FR
Cordula Hawes-Bilger, SW
Malcolm Hawes, UK
Mark Hawes, SW
Sandra Hawes, UK
Christine Hayhurst, UK
Rev Andrew Hill, UK

Lynn Hughes, USA
Rev Peter Hughes, USA
Esther Hurlburt, USA
Abigel Kiss, RO
Roslyn Maholland, USA
Eloise Mayo, USA
Rev Celia Midgley, UK
Rev John Midgley, UK
Istvan Miko, HU
Rev Orloff Miller, GE
Antje Paul, GE
Manfred Paul, GE
Rev Clifford Reed, UK
Rev Elek Rezi, RO
Barbara Smith, UK
Mark Taplin, UK
Adrienne Wilson, UK
Diane Worden, USA

Resident country legend: **FR, France; GE, Germany; HU, Hungary; RO, Romania; SW, Switzerland; UK, United Kingdom; USA, United States of America.**

APPENDIX 7

THE INTERNATIONAL COUNCIL OF UNITARIANS AND UNIVERSALISTS

— ~ —

The ICUU was founded in March 1995 at a conference in Essex, Massachusetts. It brings together national and trans-national Unitarian and Unitarian-Universalist churches, organisations and associations in over twenty countries on six continents. The ICUU's Principles and Purposes, as expressed in the Preamble to the Constitution, are as follows:

> We, the member groups of the International Council of Unitarians and Universalists, affirming our belief in religious community based on:
> - liberty of conscience and individual thought in matters of faith;
> - the inherent worth and dignity of every person;
> - justice and compassion in human relations;
> - responsible stewardship of the earth's living system;
> - and, our commitment to democratic principles,

declare our purposes to be:

- to serve the Infinite Spirit of Life and the human community by strengthening the worldwide Unitarian and Universalist faith;
- to affirm the variety and richness of our living traditions;
- to facilitate mutual support among member organisations;
- to promote our ideals and principles around the world;
- to provide models of liberal religious response to the human condition which uphold our common values.

~

SOURCE INDEX

Notes: The Source Index refers to material *attributed to* persons or organizations. It includes the range of text pages prepared by each conference contributor. For information *about* these cited sources and contributors, use the Subject Index.

Collective titles are in italics when specific authors are unknown. Parenthetical numbers following page numbers indicate multiple citations of an author on given pages. **Boldface** refers to **graphics** of various kinds.

A
Allen, Joseph Henry, 71, 95
'Ata-ur-Rahmin, Muhammad, 16, 18

B
Bainton, Roland H., 19(2), 37, 63, 95, 112(2)
translator, 100
Balázs Mihály, 25, 26, 37
Baum, Frank, 108
Baylo, Guillermo Pérez, **back cover**
Bergson, Henri, 109, 112

Bible, 60, 112, 181–82, 187
Boeke, Richard, 103–14, **120**, 124
Bolam, C. G., 60
Borbély István, 25, 26, 27, 37(3)
Bourgeois, Louis, 61
Bradford, Beatrice, **68**, **116**, 124
Bressler, Ann Lee, 56, 60
Briggs, Martin S., 60
Burns, Robert, 4–5
Buzzard, Anthony F., 29, 37

213

C
Calvin, John, 95(2)
Castellio, Sebastian, 10,
    42, 96
Channing, William Ellery,
    50, 57, 60(2)
Clifford, Sister Mary
    Dorita, 60
Crompton, Arnold, 60

D
Daniell, David, 187
Darion, Joe, 112
Dávid Ferencz., 37(4)
Deé Nagy Anna, 27, 40
Domergue, Emile, 122
Drosnin, Michael, 111,
    113

E
Ember Pál, 39
Emerson, Ralph Waldo,
    113
Erasmus, 53
Erdő János, 25, 38(2)

F
Forman, Charles C., 65
Four hundred years, 60
Friedman, Jerome, 38,
    43, 61(2), 96
Fritchman, Stephen
    Hole, 71, 96
Frothingham, Octavius
    Brooks, 69, 96–97
Fulton, John F., 71, 97

G
Gál Kelemen, 34, 38
Gavrucza Emese, 38–39
Gellérd Imre, 39
Geneva, Switzerland.
    Syndics, 188
Genevan Psalter, The,
    61
Goldstone, Lawrence, 19
Goldstone, Nancy, 19
Gordon, Alexander, 19,
    61, 122
Gordon Sándor, 39
Goring, Jeremy, 44, 61
Gospel of Thomas, The,
    181
Grant, Robert, 113
Gudmundson, V. Emil,
    61

H
Hawkes, Henry
    Warbuton, 136–44
Henry, Richard, 61
Hill, Andrew M.
    hymn, 211–12
    paper, 41–67
    Servetus monument,
        121–25
    work cited, 61–62(5)
Hillar, Marian, 71, 97
Hodges, Sir Benjamin,
    19, 191–92
Hopft, Harro, 97
Horst, I. B., 62
Hosmer, Frederick L.,
    49, 62

Hughes, Peter, 69–99
Hughes, Philip E., 97
Hunting, Charles F., 29,
    37
Hurlburt, Esther, **iv,**
    120(2), 124(2)

I
International Council of
    Unitarians and
    Universalists
    2003 conference
        attendees, 209
    2003 conference
        program, vii–viii,
        1, 23, 101, 177
    purposes and
        principles, 211–
        12
    service of commem-
        oration, 179–88

J
Jakab Elek, 25, 39
Jones, Ronald P., 61

K
Kanyró Ferencz, 39(4)
Kethe, William, 61
Kiss Áron, 39
Knox, John, 41–42, 62
Kuhn, Annette, 62

L
Lambdin, Thomas O.,
    translator, 181

Lampe, Friedrich Adolf,
    39
Lavan, Spencer, 62
Lee, Thomas Oboe, 66
Lindsey, Theophilus, 91,
    97
Long, Arthur J., 63
Longfellow, Samuel, 59,
    63
Lubienjecius, 19, 191–92

M
Marcos, Jaume de, 19
Martineau, James, 54,
    63
McAllister, Jill K., xi–xiv,
    62
McKinney, Donald W.,
    19
McLachlan, Herbert, 63
Mellone, S. H., 63
Meyer, Ronald B., 112,
    113–14
Michel Servetus Institute,
    135, 144, back
    cover
Midgley, Celia, 183–84
Morgan, John C., 63
Muir, Frederic John, 63
Mutzenberg, Gabriel, 19

N
Norman, Amandus, 64–
    64

O
Oberman, Heiko A., 88,
    97

Oelberg, Sarah, 64
Oxford Dictionary of the Christian Church, 64(2)

P
Parke, David B., 20
Parker, T. H. L., 97
Parker, Theodore, 98(2)
Patterson, George F., 64
Paul, Manfred, 64
Peaston, A. Elliott, 64
Pettegree, Andrew, 20, 65
Picasso, Pablo Ruiz, **156**
Pixis, Theodor, **135**
Porter, Philip A., 181
Priestley, Joseph, 65

R
Reed, Clifford M., xv–xxii, 62
    Champel service, 180–81, 182–83, 184–85, 186, 187
    keynote address, 3–20
    meditations, 191–205
    Servetus drama, 127–35
    Servetus sites, 115–20
Reed, Paulette, **front cover, 121,** 124
Rees, Thomas, 65

Reid, J. K. S., translator, 95
Rezi Elek, 23–40, 52
Richardson, Robert D., Jr., 65
Ritchie, Susan, 65
Robinson, James M., 187
Roper, Hugh R. Trevor, 57–58, 65
Rzepka, Jane, 145–55

S
Schachter, Zalman, 113
Scovel, Carl, 65
Sebestyén Mihály, 40
Seeing Geneva, 20, 125
Servetus, Michael
    books by, 20, 34
    quotes from, 191, 198(2), 202(2), 203, 208
    Servet Miquel aka, 39(2)–40
Servetus International Society, 156
Shakespeare, William, 204
Shelley, Percy, 106, 113
Short, H. L., 60
Sichem, Christopher, **144**
Simén Domokos, 40(3)
Singing the Living Tradition, xi, 66, 181, 186

Solomon, Norman, 112, 113
Spielman József, 27, 40
Steers, David, 66
Sütő, Andras, 157–75
Szervét könyve, 40

T
Tennyson, Alfred, Lord, 111, 113
Thomas, Roger, 60, 66
Thurman, Howard, 104–06, 113(2)
Tollin, Henrik, 36, 40
Tyndale, William, translator, 181–82, 186

V
Voltaire, 112, 113

W
Wasserman, Dale, 112
Weiss, John, 98

Wendel, François, 6, 20
Wilbur, Earl Morse, 20(2), 40, 44, 66(6)–67(2), 90, 98(2), 125
Williams, Alan, translator, 157–75
Williams, George Huntston, 25, 40, 67
Willis, Robert, 98
Wortley, F. H., 67
Wright, Conrad, 67(2), 89, 98
Wright, Richard, 71, 99
www.miguelservet.org, **135, 144, back cover**
www.multimap.com, **118,** 125
www.servetus.org, **156**

Z
Zuber, Valentine, 125

~

SUBJECT INDEX

Notes: **Boldface** page numbers in this Subject Index indicate some **drawing, graphic** or **photograph.** *Italics* refer to *artistic and literary titles* other than poems or songs as subjects.

For reference materials used by conference contributors and the text pages containing their contributions, look in the Source Index.

A

Adult baptism, 31–32, 51, 82, 107
Agh István, 34
Almási Gergely Mihaly, 36
America, 50, 75, 122
  Reformed Protestants and, 47–49, 117
  Unitarian history in, 44–45, 46, 47–49, 57, 89
  Parker and, 69, 70, 91
  Universalist history in, 45, 46, 56–57
  See also New England

Anabaptists, 45
  influence of, 50, 51
  vs. Calvinists, 31, 41–42, 168, 171
Anglicanism, 46, 48, 49, 64
Animal sacrifice, 79–80, 81–82
Antitrinitarianism, 43, 53, 92, 171
  personalities and, 25, 28, 32, 82
  See also Trinitarian doctrine; Unitarianism
Apology for Dr. Michael Servetus (Wright), 71, 99
Aragon, Spain, 123, 172
Arianism, 5–6

Arminian protests, 55, 56
Arminius, Jacobus, 54–
55, 58
Art, 49, 109, 127–35
Astrology, 7, 17
Astronomy, 16th century,
7, 17, 43, 110
Atheism, 70, 168
Atonement, 92
Austria, 32, 33, 34, 36
Awakening, The, 19th
century, 55

B
Balázs Mihály, 25, 26
Baptism, 31–32, 51, 65,
173
See also Adult
baptism; Infant
baptism
Berthelier, Philip, 86, 131
Beza, Theodore, **iv**, 119,
130
Bible
criticism and scholar-
ship in 16th
century, 5–6,
26, 29, 53, 138
criticism and scholar-
ship today, 55,
109
editions and transla-
tions, 8, 41, 53,
64, 164

Bible, *cont.*
inclusive of all
Christians, 50–
51
as inspirational, 109,
146, 155
precedence of, over
confessions of
faith, 56, 59
*See also its major
parts,* Bible.
New Testament;
Bible. Old
Testament
Bible. New Testament,
30, 31
Gospel of, and
freedom of
conscience,
123–24, 168
versions of, 5–6, 53,
108
Bible. Old Testament, 30
hymns and, 49, 113
Judaism's scriptures
as, 15, 53, 107,
110
Bible Code, The
(Drosnin), 111, 113
Bishops, 46, 47
Bishops, Transylvanian,
33–34
Bishop's Palace, 9, 116,
116, 118
Blandrata, Georgio, 32–
33

Boeke, Richard, xx
  See also Source
    Index
Borbély István, scholar-
  ship of, 25, 26, 27
British Isles, 48, 55, 91,
  122
  *See also specific
    countries*
Buddhism, adherents of,
  124
Bunyan, Linda, 184
Burns, Robert, 4–5

C
Cain, Cynthia, 180, 185
Calvin, Antoine, 81
Calvin, John, 9, **135**
  accusations against,
    5–6, 35, 151,
    155
  attitudes toward, 42–
    43, 46–47, 70,
    93, 94, 112
  doctrines of, 30, 42,
    48, 54–58, 59,
    82, 128, 175
  as dramatic character,
    130–32, 134,
    136–43, 153–
    54, 158–75
  faithful lieutenants of,
    iv, 3, 4, 31, 119
  human nature and,
    13, 54

Calvin, John, *cont.*
  legacy to U / U's from,
    42, 47–55, 59,
    70, 89–90
  monuments to, **iv,**
    117, 119, **120,**
    123
  pulpit of, 117, 168–74
  role in Servetus's trial,
    81, 82, 85, 104,
    129
  variant names of, 7,
    122, 157
  works, 111, 151, 159
Calvinism
  bibliophile adherents
    of, 34–36
  contributions of, 50–
    52, 87
  founders of, 3, 119
  theology of, 29, 46,
    56, 57–58, 89
  Unitarian protests
    against, 54–58,
    70
Cambridge Platform
  (1648), 48
Čapek, Norbert, 45
Caroli, Petrus, 5
Castellio, Sebastian, 10,
    54, 90, 96, 164
Cathédrale St-Pierre,
    116, 117, **118**
Catholicism. *See* Roman
    Catholic Church

Central America, fledging
U / U groups in,
45–46
Champel, Geneva, **118**
commemorative
service at, 179–
88
as execution site, 9,
79, 119, 122,
123, 129
procession to, 79, 117
Servetus monument
near, 119, 122
Champs du Bourreau,
Geneva, 122
Channing, William Ellery,
50–51, 57
Children, 13, 51, 71
infant baptism for, 31,
32
Christianismi Restitutio
(Servetus), 17, 171
Dávid and, 27–28,
32–33
extant copies of, 9,
32, 33
as inspirational
resource, 111,
182–83, 191,
198, 202
publication or
reprinting of, 8–
9, 33, 35–36,
128, 151–52

Christianismi Restitutio
(Servetus), *cont.*
purchase and
ownership
transfer of, 33–
36
Christianity, 85, 88
branches of (*see
specifics, e.g.,*
Anglicanism;
General
Baptists;
Lutheranism;
Reformed
Protestant
tradition;
Roman Catholic
Church)
creeds of, 5–6, 36,
67, 89
events in Jesus's life
interpreted by,
46, 74, 106, 107
movements in history,
55, 56, 57
Reformations in, 139
Catholic, 6, 9, 128,
147–48,
165–66
Protestant, 3, 4, 9,
41, 47, 70,
117, 148
Radical, 6–7, 13,
18, 25, 148–
49, 160
See also Trinitarian
doctrine

Christology. *See* Jesus
 Christ
Church, The, as entity,
 106
 one true holy, 59, 96,
  152
 separate from society,
  50–52, 59, 87–
  88
Church architecture, U /
 U, 41, 49–50, 59,
 64
Church of England. *See*
 Anglicanism
Clement VII, 128, 147
"Cloud, The" (Shelley),
 106–7
Communion. *See* Lord's
 Supper, The
Communities
 historical sacrifice in,
  and U / U's, 78–
  82, 89–93
 purification of, 82, 85–
  86, 92
 sacrifice and, 73–78,
  82, 84–87, 88,
  92–94
Comparative religion,
 sacrifice in, 73
Congregational
 governance
 actions by, 36, 86–87
 models of, 47, 48, 59
Conscience, 13, 160
 freedom of, 91, 123–
  24, 133

Conscience, *cont.*
 right of, 17, 18, 134,
  174
Consistories. *See*
 Congregational
 governance
Courage, witness for
 truth and, 95, 129
Creation
 pre-existence of
  Christ from, 29–
  30
 theology and, 26, 108,
  111
Creative Evolution
 (Bergson), 109
Creeds, rejection of, 93
Crisis theologies, in 20th
 century
 Christianity, 55
Cromwell, Oliver, 117
Czechoslovak Church,
 45

D
Dance, U / U worship
 and, 49
Dávid, Francis. *See*
 Dávid Ferencz
Dávid Ferencz, 45
 beliefs of, 30, 51
 *Christianismi
  Restitutio* and,
  27–28, 32–33
 life events of, 33, 46
 Servetus's influence
  on, 23–28

Dávid Ferencz, *cont.*
  Servetus's influence
    on, denied, 25–
    26
  Servetus's influence
    on, re-evalu-
    ated, 28–32
  works, 27, 30
De Baptisma Officiae
  (Servetus), 31
de Benneville, George,
  46
De Haereticis (Castellio),
  10
De Murr, Cristoph, 33–34
De Ordine Mysterium
  Regenerationis
  (Servetus), 31–32
De Regno Antichristi
  liber secundus
  (Dávid), 27, 30
De Regno Christi liber
  primus (Dávid), 27
De Trinitatis Erroribus
  (Servetus), 5, 108,
  128, 149, 202
de Villeneuve, Michel.
  See Servetus,
  Michael
Deutsche Katholicismus,
  45
Deutsche Unitaria
  Religionsgemein-
  schaft, 184

Devil, The, 108
  machinations of, 14,
    84, 96, 155
  Servetus possessed
    by, 79, 149
Dialogorum de Trinitate
  Libri Duo
  (Servetus), 5
Diary of Catalina
  Conesa, The
  (Rzepka), 133,
  145–55
Dissenters, religious, 54,
  55–56, 59
Divine Spirit. *See* Holy
  Spirit
Domergue, Emile, 122
Dramas about Servetus,
  127–35
  The Diary of Catalina
    Conesa
    (Rzepka), 133,
    145–55
  film scenario
    proposal, 127–
    29
  Flames at the Stake
    (Sütõ), 133–35,
    157–75
  Servetus: A Drama
    (Hawkes), 130–
    32, 136–44
Dutch Remonstrant
  Brotherhood, 55

E

Eastern Europe. *see specific countries or regions, e.g., Hungary; Poland; Romania; Transylvania*

Ecumenical conspiracies, 16th century, 6, 9, 17, 32, 150, 154

Edit of Toleration (1781), 34

Educational institutions, 36, 52, 53–54, 122

Edward VI (king of England), 4

Edwards, Jonathan, 70

Emerson, Ralph Waldo, 45, 110

England, 33, 45
  Church of (*see* Anglicanism)
  exiles from, 41, 47–48, 93, 117
  monarchies in, 4, 48
  Protestant Reformation in, 4, 41, 47–48, 117
  religious cruelties in, 4, 71
  Unitarian Universalism in, 57
  church architecture, 41, 50

England,
  Unitarian Universalism in, *cont.*
  colleges, 54, 122
  history, 44, 46, 47–49

Episcopalian Christianity. *see* Anglicanism

Erasmus, 5–6, 27, 53

Errors
  Calvin's era and, 79, 104, 123, 159
  On the, of the Trinity (Servetus), 5, 108, 128, 149, 202

Europe, 17–18, 56, 57, 117, 158
  Catholicism in, 32, 34, 41, 128
  See also specific countries

European Unitarian Universalists, 184

Évêché, L'. *See* Bishop's Palace

Excommunication, 86

F

Faith
  formal Confessions of, 48, 55
  God and, 110, 111
  Unitarian Universalists and, 3, 10–18, 50–52

Farel, Guillaume
    as character in
        Servetus
        drama, 134–35,
        158, 165, 168,
        170, 171–72,
        174–75
    Genevan sites related
        to, **iv**, 115, **118,**
        119
    Servetus's theological
        errors and, 79,
        104
Father, Son and Holy
    Ghost, 10–11, 31,
    108
    See also separately,
        God; Holy Spirit;
        Jesus Christ
Feminists, 45
Flames at the Stake
    (Sütõ), 133–35,
    157–75
Fontaine, Nicolas de la.
    See La Fontaine,
    Nicolas de
Forgiveness, 14, 181
Fox, George, 110
Fox, Matthew, 108
France, 71, 121
    Catholics in, 32, 81,
        84, 85
    Inquisition, 4, 81,
        130, 157–58
    Schweitzer–Servetus
        connection in,
        107–8

France, *cont.*
    Servetus studied in,
        104, 128, 146
    Vienne, 127, 130
    Servetus resided
        in, 8, 80, 81,
        150
    works published or
        written in, 57,
        129, 149
Francis, Convers, 70
Free Thinkers, 19th
    century, 121
Freedom. *See* Religious
    freedom
Friedman, Jerome, 24–
    25, 43, 72

G
Gál Kelemen, 34
Gandhi, Mahatma
        Mohandas, 105–6
Gelei Katona István, 29
General Assembly of
    Unitarians and
    Free Christian
    Churches, 184
General Baptists, 45, 51,
    107
Geneva, Lake
    (Switzerland). *See*
    Leman, Lac
    (Switzerland)
Geneva, Switzerland, 3,
    41, 55, 69
    Calvin's era in, 4, 8,
        10, 32, 36, **44,**

Geneva, Switzerland,
Calvin's era in, *cont.*
68, 81–87, 94,
115–16, 161–65
governing council and
syndic of, 78,
81, 82–84, 85–
87, 122–24,
131, 172, 174–
75, 188
Servetus in, 9, 79–80,
86, 103–4, 115–
19
as setting for dramas,
129, 131–32,
136, 140, 157,
168
sites to visit, 9–10,
115–19, 118,
120–21, 121–24
Genevan city streets
av. Beau-Séjour, 118,
119, 122–23,
124, 125
av. de la Rosarie,
118, 119, 122,
124, 125
Place du Molard, 9,
115, 118
Place Neuve, 117
rue de la Croix
Rouge, 117,
118
rue de l'Évêché, 116,
118
rue du Rhône, 9, 115,
118

Genevan city streets,
cont.
rue Michel-Servet,
118, 119, 120,
122, 124, 125,
185
rue St-Antoine, 79
Genevan Psalter tunes,
49, 61, 207
Geography, 43, 150
Ptolemy and, 8, 17
Germany, 57, 128
*Christianismi
Restitutio* copy
in, 32, 35–38
religious movements
in, 45, 46, 150,
165
God, 14
Commonwealth of
(*see subentry
below,* Kingdom
of)
creedal doctrine of, 5,
6, 89
honouring the purity
of, 81, 85–86
Kingdom of, 88, 110,
111
metaphors for, 104–7
nature of, 12–13, 31,
57, 70, 108, 111
non-Christian views
of, 16, 104, 106
Word of, 49, 53–54

God, *cont.*
  See also Trinitarian
    doctrine; Unity
    of God
Greek culture
  drama masks, 108
  language, 5, 53, 108
  philosophy, 29, 109,
    175
  religion, 81, 106
Guild, Polly, 133, 145

H
Hapsburg Empire,
  Catholic court of,
    34
Harris Manchester
  College, Oxford, 54
Harvard College,
  Massachusetts, 54
Harvard University,
  library, 36
Harvey, William, 17, 110
Hawkes, Henry
  Warburton, 130
Hayhurst, Christine,
  182–83, 186
Henry VIII (king of
  England), 4
Heretics, 70, 107
  aliases used by, 8,
    157
  Castellio's work, 10,
    96

Heretics, *cont.*
  condemnation of, 9,
    36, 82, 116,
    155, 188
  orthodox Christians
    and, 4–5, 6, 80,
    85, 171–72
Heroism, 94–95
Hill, Andrew M., xx, 89,
  181–82
Hinduism, 104, 106
History of Unitarianism
  (Wilbur), 44
Holy Ghost. *See* Holy
  Spirit
Holy Spirit, 30, 31, 107,
  110
  as disposition rather
    than as person
    of God, 10–11,
    11–12, 108
  in Jesus and other
    humans, 12, 13,
    108
Hôtel de Ville, 78, 117,
  118
Hughes, Peter, xx–xxi
  See also Source
    Index
Humanists, 45, 53, 158
Humankind
  nature of, 13–14, 54,
    89
  public responsibility
    for, 50–52, 59
  spirit of, 12, 13

Hungary, 23, 57, 133
    Calvinist theology in,
        29, 46
    ethnic historians of
        Transylvanian
        Unitarianism,
        25, 26
    See also Transylvania
Hunted Heretic
    (Bainton), 109
Hus, Jan, 70, 104
Huss, John. *See* Hus,
    Jan
Hymns, 58–59, 106, 113,
    207–8

I
Icelandic Unitarian
    churches, 46
ICUU. *See* International
    Council of
    Unitarians and
    Universalists
Iglesia Filipina
    Independiente, 45
India, 57, 105–6
Infant baptism
    Servetus rejected, 84,
        107, 155
    U / U substitute for,
        51
    vs. adult baptism, 31,
        32, 82
Innocence, 13
Inquisition. *See under*
    Roman Catholic
    Church

Inspirational resources
    Bible, 113, 146, 155
    *Christianismi
        Restitutio*
        (Servetus), 111,
        182–83, 191,
        198, 202
    clouds, 106–7
    commemorative
        service for
        Michael
        Servetus, 179–
        88
    legacies from Michael
        Servetus, 58–
        59, 93, 94–95,
        107
    "Michael's
        Meditations"
        (Reed), 191–
        205
    *Institutes of the Christian
        Religion* aka
        *Instituto
        Christianismi*
        (Calvin), 95, 111,
        151, 159
    International Council of
        Unitarians and
        Universalists
        (ICUU)
        commemorative
            service by, 119,
            124, 179–88
        conferences
            2001 Oxford, 52,
            54

International Council of
Unitarians and
Universalists
(ICUU),
conferences, *cont.*
2003 Geneva, vii–
viii, xv, 184,
209
essence and promise
of, xi–xiv
See also Source
Index
Ireland, 50, 55, 71
Islam, 14–15, 56, 103,
111, 152
See also Qur'an
Italy, 71, 128, 154

J

Jakubec, Rev. Marie-
Laure, **120,** 186
János Zsigmond, 32
Jesus Christ, 6, 16, 31
Lord's Supper
controversy
about, 46, 107
nature of, 11–12, 14,
26, 43
pre-existence of, 29–
30
Jesus in history, 70, 110
life events of, 74, 103,
106, 153
Servetus's belief in,
147, 155

Jesus in history, *cont.*
as Son of God in his
lifetime, 104,
108
Joan of Arc, 104
Joseph II (holy Roman
emperor), 34, 36
Judaism, 105, 107
clouds as inspiration
in, 106–7
conversion of Jews in
Spain, 56, 152–
53
21st century wars
and, 103, 111
sympathies for, 14–15
See also Bible. Old
Testament;
Talmud
Judgment Day, 13, 147,
186

K

Khasi Hills, India, 57
King, Martin Luther, Jr.,
104–5
King's Chapel, Boston,
46
"Kirk's Alarm, The"
(Burns), 4–5
Kiss, Abigel, 184
Knox, John, **iv,** 3, 4, 9,
41–42, 119
Koran. *See* Qur'an

L

La Fontaine, Nicolas de, 81, 172
Lake Geneva (Switzerland). *See* Leman, Lac (Switzerland)
Language instruction, 53–54
Lázár Istvan, 34
Legacies to U / U's
  from Calvin, 42, 47–55, 59, 70, 94
  from Reformed Protestant tradition, 54
  from Servetus, 58–59, 93, 94–95, 107
Leman, Lac (Switzerland), **68**, 115, **118**
Liberal church, 66, 72, 88, 92
Libertines, 86–87, 159, 161
Libraries, 36
Lindsey, Theophilus, 46
Lord's Supper, The, 46, 51, 66, 85, 107
Luther, Martin, as character in drama, 160, 166, 168
Lutheranism, 46, 168

M

Marriage, as ordinance, 52

Martineau, James, 54
Mary I, Tudor (queen of England), 4, 41
Massachusetts Commonwealth, 48, 53–54, 70
McAllister, Jill K., xxi
  See also Source Index
Meaning, 17, 73–74, 93–94, 109
Medicine, 17
  frontiers of 16th century, 43, 110, 150–51
  hospital areas for, **68**, **116, 118**, 119, 122
Memorials to Servetus.
  See Servetus memorials; Servetus monuments
Metaphysical proofs, avoidance of, 29
Midgley, Celia, 187–88
Miko, Istvan, 184
Miller, Orloff, 184
Ministers, 55
  legacies from Reformed tradition to, 47, 48, 53–54, 59
  as participants in commemorative service, 180–84, 185–86

Ministers, *cont.*
  as playwrights, 130,
    133, 145
  See also specifics,
    e.g., Calvin,
    John; Farel,
    Guillaume
Minor Reformed Church,
    Poland, 47
Monotheism, 10, 14–16,
    18
Monument de la
    Réformation, **iv**,
    117–119, **118**
Monuments to Servetus.
    See Servetus
    memorials;
    Servetus
    monuments
Murray, John, 56
Music in U / U societies
  "Gathered Here," 181,
    186
  Genevan Psalter
    heritage of, 49,
    61, 207
  hymns about
    Servetus, 58–
    59, 207–8
  "The Impossible
    Dream," 110,
    112
Myths, 76, 89–93

N
Nature, universals in, 13,
    106, 108, 109–10

Netherlands, The, 27,
    55, 71
New England, America,
    48, 50, 51, 117
North Africa, Servetus in,
    15
North America, 46, 55,
    117
  See also America
Norwegian Unitarian
    churches, 46

O
Oecolompadius,
    Johannes, 7, 139
"Old Hundredth"
    (Genevan Psalter),
    49, 61
"Old 124th" *(Genevan*
    Psalter), 207
Origen, 70
Original sin, 14, 56–57,
    92
Orthodox Christians
  challenges and, 70,
    128
  separation from, 4–5,
    9, 18, 93, 129
  16th-century
    scholarship and,
    6–7
  superiority of, 15, 71
  Unitarian groups and,
    45, 89

P
Pagans, 45

231

Pagnini Bible, 8
Pálffy Zsigmond, 34
Panentheism, 12–13, 18, 108
Pantheism, 12–13, 168, 171
Parker, Theodore, 69–70, 71, 91
Paul, Antje, 184
Paul, Manfred, 184
Paul (the apostle), 70, 174
Pelagius, 70
Perrin, Amy, 131, 134, 170
Pietism, Lutheran, 46
Piety, Christ and, 96
Plato, 29, 175
Poetry, U / U worship and, 49
Poland, religion in, 45, 47, 48–49, 51, 53
Political governance, 131, 145, 147
Prayer, 79, 105, 184–85
Preaching, 110
    Calvin's sermon topics, 117, 169–74
    as central to worship, 49–50, 59
Predestination doctrine, 54–55, 59
Priestley, Joseph, 45, 56–57

Prisons
    Bishop's Palace among, 116, **116**
    Servetus in, 78, 117, 131–32, 154, 155
Promenade des Bastions, Geneva, **iv,** 117
Proof texts, Bible as, 5–6, 29
Protestant Reformation
    challenges to, 9, 148–49
    ecumenical conspiracies of, 6, 8–9, 17, 32, 150, 154
    England and the, 4, 41, 47–48, 117
    Genevan model and, 5–6, 49, 117
Psalters, as U / U music heritage, 49, 61, 207
Public responsibility, 50–52, 59, 81, 110
Pulmonary circulation, 7, 17, 104, 110
Purification of communities, 85–86, 92
Puritans, 47–48, 93, 117

Q
Quakerism, 110

Qur'an, 15, 25–26

R
Racovians, 51, 53
Radical Reformation, 69, 93
    as challenge to rival orthodoxies, 97, 127–28, 148–49, 160
Rational inquiry or thought. *See* Reason
Reason, 110, 155, 174
    absence of, and violence, 103, 111–12
    truth uncovered by, 17, 18, 54
    as Unitarian principle, 59, 87, 90
Reed, Clifford M., xxi, **120,** 180–81, 186
    See also Source Index
Reformed Protestant tradition
    Catholic criticism and, 84, 85
    Genevan monuments raised by, 117, 119, **120–21,** 121–24, 125
    heterodox *vs.* orthodox similarities in, 47, 49–50, 89

Reformed Protestant tradition, *cont.*
    principles of, 50–52, 59, 123–24
    struggle between, and radicalism, 54–58, 93
    Unitarian heritage in, 49–54, 59
Religious disasters, 71, 88, 96, 165
Religious freedom
    in Calvin's era, 161–62, 168
    as issue, 10, 18, 37, 59
    pioneers of, 70, 104
    in Servetus's case, 42, 172, 175
    as Unitarian principle, 90–91, 92
Religious liberals, 88
    defence of, 4–5
    issues for, 10, 17, 18, 59
    Servetus as precursor to, 91–92
Religious Society of Czech Unitarians, 45
Relly, James, 56
Réveil, Le, 19th century, 55
Revivalists, 56
Rezi Elek, xxi–xxii
    See also Source Index

Rhône River, 8, **44**
Rigot, Claude, 81
Roman Catholic Church,
    109
  doctrines of, 5–6, 15,
    153
  ecumenical
    conspiracies of,
    6, 8–9, 17, 32,
    150, 154
  in Europe, 32, 34, 41,
    128
  Inquisition of, 4, 8, 15,
    81, 115, 152–
    53, 154, 157–58
  Mass as sacramental
    heritage of, 49,
    107
  Protestant Reformed
    church criticized
    by, 84–85, 121
  Reformation of, 6,
    128, 147–48,
    165–66
  Unitarian groups with
    origins in, 45–
    46, 58
Romania, 36, 133
  See also Transylvania
Rose d'Or, La
    (business), 9, 115,
    118
Ruach Hagofen, 105,
    106
Rzepka, Jane, 134, 145

S
Sacrifice
  community purifica-
    tion with, 85–86
  definitions, 73, 77
  historical, 73–77, 78–
    79, 88–93
  ritual, 73, 78–88
  Servetus as, 71, 77–
    93, 94–95
  signs of consent in,
    80–81
Sadoleto, Cardinal
    Jacopo, 83
St. Giles Cathedral,
    Edinburgh, 9
St. Paul. *See* Paul (the
    apostle)
St. Peter's Cathedral,
    Geneva. *See*
    Cathédrale St-
    Pierre
Salter's Hall controversy,
    55, 56
Salvation, 14, 55, 152
  universal, 13, 56–57
Satan. *See* Devil, The
Savoyards, 82–83, 164
Scholarship, 8–9, 26
  biblical, in 16th
    century, 5–6,
    53–54
  object of, 18, 109
Schweitzer, Albert, 107–
    8
Science, 17, 43, 109

Scotland, 43, 71
  Calvinist Reformation
    in, 3, 41
  extant copy of *Chris-
    tianismi Resti-
    tutio* in, 9, 32
Scriptures. *See* Bible;
  Qur'an
Seders, 107
Servetus: A Drama
  (Hawkes), 130–32,
  136–44
Servetus, Michael, **144**
  accusations against,
    70, 78–79, 81,
    82, 102, 107
    (*see also subentry
      below,*
      teachings)
  attitudes toward, 36,
    41–42, 80–81,
    84, 128, 149–50
  characteristics of, 6,
    8, 15–17, 43,
    69, 70, 94, 109,
    128, 129
  Dávid and, re-eval-
    uated, 28–32
  excepted from
    Unitarianism,
    24–25, 43, 67,
    72
  influence of, 10–18,
    26–28, 45, 58–
    59, 70, 71, 96

Servetus, Michael, *cont.*
  occupations of, 7–8,
    17–18, 109,
    128, 150–51
  Parker's view of, 69–
    70, 71
  as sacrifice, 71, 77–
    93, 94–95
  teachings, 37, 43, 92,
    107–11, 172–
    74, 186
    (*see also subentry
      above,*
      accusations
      against)
  variant names of, 3, 5,
    7, 123, 153, 157
  works, 28, 31–36, 79,
    155
    *De Baptisma
      Officiae,* 31
    *On the Errors of
      the Trinity,* 5,
      107–8, 128,
      149, 202
    letters and other
      writings, 203
    *On the Order of
      Renewal of
      Sacraments,*
      31–32
    *The Restoration of
      Christianity*
      (*see its main
      entry,*
      Christianismi

Servetus, Michael,
  works, *cont.*
    Restitutio
    (Servetus))
    Syruporum
      Universa
      Ratio, 7, 150
    *Two Dialogues on
      the Trinity, 5*
    See also under,
    Inspirational
      resources
Servetus, Michael, life
  events of
  arrests, 9, 79, 116,
    128, 130, 155
  early years, 15, 104,
    123, 128, 133,
    145–46
  escapes or flights, 7,
    9, 80, 115, 128,
    129, 130, 154,
    158
  imprisonments, 78,
    116, **116,** 131–
    32, **135,** 154,
    155, **156**
  martyrdom, 9, 18, 27,
    43, 58, 71, 79,
    94, 103–4, 155,
  schooling, 104, 128,
    146
  time in Geneva, 9–10,
    79–80, 86–87,
    103–4, 115–19
  trials, 79, 81, 82, 104,
    129, 154, 172

Servetus memorials
  anniversary books,
    xx–xxi, 5
  flowers, 124, 186
  hymns, 58–59, 207–8
  namesake societies,
    xix, 58, 144
  service of commem-
    oration, 119,
    179–88
Servetus monuments
  American proposal
    for, 70
  Genevan, **front
    cover, 118,**
    119, **120–21,**
    121–24, 125
  other European, 121
Shelley, Percy, 106
Sin and sinfulness, 14,
    56, 81, 92
Singh, Hajom Kissor, 57
Smith, Barbara, 184
Socinus, Faustus, 43, 70
  influence of, 51, 55,
    58, 65, 89
Son and Holy Ghost, 10–
    11, 11–12, 108
  See also separately,
    Holy Spirit;
    Jesus Christ
Souls, 93, 107
  "inner light" as, 110,
    142–43
  trapped by Satan, 84,
    96

South America, fledging
U / U groups in,
45–46
Spain
art about Servetus
from, 129, 156,
back cover
Christianity in, 56, 71
Inquisition
persecutions,
14–15, 152–
53
fledging U / U groups
in, 45–46
foremost native of, 69,
121
Servetus's early years
in, 14–15, 104,
123, 128, 133,
145–46
State, The, as entity, 87–
88
Stroudinsky, Rt. Rev.
Joel, **120,** 186
Sütő, Andras, 133
Switzerland, 33, 128
cities in, 81, 82–83,
83, 165
(*see also* Geneva,
Switzerland)
Reformation in, 47,
48–49, 82
religious cruelties in,
71, 180–81, 191
Synods. *See*
Congregational
governance

Syria, child sacrifice in,
71
Syruporum Universa
Ratio (Servetus), 7,
150
Szentábrahámi Lombárd
Mihály, 34
Szentiványi Márcos
Dániel, 33, 36

T
Talmud, independence
from, 25–26
Teleki Count Samuel,
34–36
Temple de la Madeleine,
9, 80, 115–16, **118**
Theological School,
Geneva, 36
Thurman, Howard, 104–
6
Tolerance
as issue for religious
liberals, 10, 18,
37, 59, 90–91
religious persecution
vs, 121
religious persecution
vs., 71
Transcendentalists, 45
Transubstantiation, 107
Transylvania, 32–33, 36,
46
Transylvanian
Unitarianism
baptism as ordinance,
31–32

Transylvanian
  Unitarianism, *cont.*
    bishops in, 33–34
    church architecture in
      Koloszvar, 49–
        50
    education and, 52, 53
    Hungarian historians
      and, 25, 26
    Reformed tradition in,
      47, 48–49, 49–
        50, 56
    Servetus and history
      of, 25–26, 33–
        36, 37
Trinitarian doctrine
  Dávid and, 29, 43
  as interfaith barrier,
    15–16
  orthodox insistence
    upon, 6, 11, 15,
      89, 104, 175
  Roman Catholic
    teaching of, 5,
      108, 153
  Trinity of Persons, **5,**
    6, **11,** 56, 89,
      104, 112
  See also Antitrini-
    tarianism
Truth, 6
  search for, 17, 18, 26,
    27, 37.
  witness for, 95, 103,
    129, 143–44,
      175

U
U / U's. *See* Unitarian
  Universalists
Unitarian Church of
  Hungary, 184
Unitarian Church of
  Romania, 184
Unitarian Home
  Missionary
  College,
  Manchester, 122
Unitarian Universalist
  Association (UUA),
    58–59, 184
Unitarian Universalist
  Church of the
  Philippines, 45–46
Unitarian Universalists
  (U / U's)
    faith of, 10–18, 185
    historical sacrifice in
      community of,
        78–79, 88–93
    history of their ideas
      vs. their people,
        44–59
    myths for, 89–93
    principles of, 17, 18,
      50–52, 59, 90–
        92, 94–95
    as representative of
      the Liberal
      church, 72, 88
    resistance to Calvin's
      legacy by, 42,
        54–57, 92, 93

Unitarian Universalists
(U / U's), *cont.*
See also International
Council of
Unitarians and
Universalists
(ICUU);
Unitarianism;
Universalism
Unitarianism
Calvin's legacy to, 42,
47–54, 59, 89,
94
Calvin's theology
protested by
adherents of,
54–57
Catholic origins for
some groups
within, 45–46,
58
English churches and,
41, 49, 50
heterodoxy of, 43, 89
ordinances of, 51–52,
65, 66
Theodore Parker and,
69, 70, 91
Servetus as pioneer
of, 10, 17, 44,
70, 96, 107
Servetus excepted
from, 24–25, 43,
72
sympathies for, 4–5

Unitarianism, *cont.*
See also
Transylvanian
Unitarianism;
Unitarian
Universalists
(U / U's)
United States of
America. *See*
America
Unity of God, 12, 138
all-inclusive mindset
reflected in, 50–
51
faith in, as all Reality,
111, 185
independent
conclusions on,
26, 28
in monotheism, 10, 43
Universalism, 13, 17, 46,
51, 56–57
See also Unitarian
Universalists
(U / U's)
Universe, 13, 106, 109,
110
UUA. *See* Unitarian
Universalist
Association

V
Violence
acceptance of, 48,
81–82, 85

Violence, *cont*
  disagreement no
    excuse for, 42,
    173
  disagreement without,
    16–17, 91
  religious disasters as,
    71, 88, 96, 165
  sacrificial killings as
    non-criminal,
    75–88
  Voltaire on, 112, 113–
    14
  wars with, 48, 103,
    111–12
Vitéz József, 36
Voltaire, 3

W
Wales, 47–48, 57
Wanstall, Mme.
  Marianne, **120,** 186

Western culture, 69, 103,
  109, 158
  See also Greek
    culture
*Westminster Confession
  of Faith* (Church of
  England), 48, 89
Williams, Roger, 117
Winter's Tale, The
  (Shakespeare),
  204
Wizard of Oz, The
  (Baum), 108
Word of God, 49, 53–54
Worship, U / U, 49, 59
Wright, Frank Lloyd, 50

Z
Zara (business), 115,
  118

~